ReViewing the Movies

Focal Point Series
ReViewing the Movies:
A Christian Response to Contemporary Film
by Peter Fraser and Vernon Edwin Neal

Christians in a .com World:
Getting Connected Without Getting Consumed
by Gene Edward Veith, Jr. and Chris Stamper

FOCAL POINT SERIES

Gene Edward Veith, Jr., general editor

ReViewing the Movies

A Christian Response to Contemporary Film

Peter Fraser
& Vernon Edwin Neal

CROSSWAY BOOKS • WHEATON, ILLINOIS
A DIVISION OF GOOD NEWS PUBLISHERS

ReViewing the Movies: A Christian Response to Contemporary Film

Copyright © 2000 by Peter Fraser and Vernon Edwin Neal

Published by Crossway Books
        a division of Good News Publishers
        1300 Crescent Street
        Wheaton, Illinois 60187

Cover design: David LaPlaca

Cover photo: PhotoDisc™

First printing 2000

Printed in the United States of America

Library of Congress Cataloging-in-Publication Data
Fraser, Peter, 1957–
   Reviewing the movies : a Christian response to contemporary film / Peter Fraser and Vernon Edwin Neal.
      p.   cm. — (Focal point series)
   Includes biographical references and index.
   ISBN 1-58134-203-9 (pbk.)
   1. Motion pictures in Christian education. 2. Motion pictures—Moral and ethical aspects. 3. Motion pictures—Reviews. 4. Motion pictures—Religious aspects—Christianity. 5. Christian life. I. Neal, Vernon Edwin, 1950– II. Title. III. Series.
   BV1535.4.F73   2000
   261.5'7—dc21   00-008984
                                                                    CIP

15	14	13	12	11	10	09	08	07	06	05	04	03	02	01	00
15	14	13	12	11	10	9	8	7	6	5	4	3	2	1

To Martha, my beloved wife,
and to our dear children—Amberlea,
Cole, Emily, and Maggie.
I will love you forever.
Peter Fraser

This book is dedicated to the two special
women in my life—my late grandmother
Ida Mae New and my mother Elizabeth Boyd.
Vernon Edwin Neal

Contents

Buster Keaton, *The General* (1927). This and all other photographs in this book are used by permission of the Wisconsin Center for Film and Theater Research.

Acknowledgments

PETER FRASER

I am grateful to have had the opportunity to work with my insightful and kind friend Vernon Edwin Neal, without whom this project would never have happened. Thanks also to Ed Veith and to Marvin Padgett of Crossway Books for their help in getting this book out. And to my good friend Arthur Livingston, as always.

I am most in the debt of my beloved wife, Martha, for steady love and encouragement (Song of Songs 2:2).

VERNON EDWIN NEAL

Special thanks to God for the strength and ability He grants, and to Arthur C. New, Ethel Gintoff, Anne Blair, James L. Limbacher, Richard Voss, Pastor Dennis Kleist, Frank Blake, Christine and Jerry Laird, Stanley Johnson, Albert Ritsema, Val Albrecht, Sam Williams, Joyce and Marshall Flasher, Roger Westphal, Rev. Kim R. Taylor, and Dr. Peter Fraser, whose friendship, support, and talent made this project a great experience.

Introduction:
In Pursuit of Consistency

The subject of this little book is our relationship as Christians to one of the most powerful cultural influences in America, the cinema. Film is a detail in the arena of our recreations, one of those in which a combination of ignorance and lack of training has insulated us in many ways from the tender influences of God's Spirit. A split that began in colleges and universities between Christianity and "learned subjects" has left most of us with no idea what a Christian approach to a subject like film might be, and perhaps very little interest in finding out.

We are part of a culture that falls in love with our entertainments first and thinks about them later. If we like a particular film, we find a justification for our affection. Consequently, like teenagers, we bond to half-formed ideas and second-rate art and ignore in many cases the good, true, and beautiful (cf. Philippians 4:8). To understand through a word picture, think of some poor father trying to convince his son to get to know some genuinely wonderful young girl, but the son resists, his heart set on an unattainable beauty queen. The beauty queen has a better complexion and rounder calves and a cleverer way of expression—qualities that the inexperienced son holds without doubt to be ingredients of happy marriage and family life. The father, knowing better from hard experience, groans in his spirit that his son has turned off his mind to satisfy his deluded heart. We American Christians are, of course, like the son—led by cultural convention and undeveloped taste and judgment to embrace the idols of the crowd. We, by and large, watch the same movies, read stories of the stars in the same popular rags, await the same promotions, applaud the same awards. Like the Father He is, God must groan at the situation.

I taught a student recently who saw the film *Titanic* seven times. This was a fine Christian girl by all estimations. So I wondered, what is the attraction of the film for a girl like this? The special effects are impressive. The historical subject has some continuing appeal—there is indeed here an age-old moral lesson in the story of human pride leading to calamity. The visuals are in some scenes beautiful. But I soon ran out of good explanations and started thinking of possible bad ones. (Seven viewings after all.) She wants that self-confidence and brashness that throws the most precious jewel in the world into the sea. She finds Leonardo DiCaprio attractive. She wants an artist to sketch her portrait in the nude.

Actually, the only reason any person, let alone a young Christian girl, would see a film like *Titanic* seven times is that the world of that film is the world that person really wants to be a part of. The problem, of course, for a follower of Jesus is that the world of that film is only marginally, peripherally a Christian world.

In saying this, I am not referring to the film's rating or its quotient of violent and sexual content, as this book will go on to show. I am referring to its messages, both explicit and implicit. But I don't want to pick on *Titanic*, for there are far worse popular films.

The problem is less "the films out there" than it is our collective lack of judgment produced by a lack of training. We don't know how to measure and evaluate film from a Christian point of view. We hardly know what a Christian point of view is toward art, unless we think of counting swear words and body parts or start looking for the presence of Christian characters.

Paul tells us to do all things to God's glory—eating, drinking, playing basketball. Unsure of how to go about doing that, we unwrap the text through little rules like "I pray before each meal" or "I won't drink beer or smoke cigarettes" (cigars being okay). When it comes to movies, we draw little lines in the sand—"I won't ever see *Last Tango in Paris* because it's about bad people having illicit sex, but it's acceptable to see *Titanic* seven times because its about nice people having illicit sex." The problem in America can be blamed in part on how we have been trained to think about "religious issues."

Recently I heard a lecture in which the speaker argued that the loss of faith in so many once-Christian colleges and universities—think of Stanford, Harvard, or Duke—can be traced to the evolving belief of the last few centuries that religion should be taught separately from academic subjects like science and math and the arts. In plain terms, academic policy in American schools of higher learning has come to determine that in one room we learn about atomic particles or integers, while in another we learn about God.

George Marsden has documented the history of this schism between Christianity and the subjects we study in school, opening his argument in *The Outrageous Idea of Christian Scholarship* with the observation that "contemporary university culture is hollow at its core." By this Marsden condemns the situation we have, even in colleges and universities with church affiliations, whereby it is thought an intrusion to discuss Christianity as an intellectual or philosophical worldview bearing on whatever else we learn or do. Marsden is, of course, correct in this. Without Christ as the center of discussion, intellectual pursuits do prove hollow.

As Christians we must confess that God declares Himself through electrons and prime numbers. Read Psalm 19: "The heavens declare the glory of God. . . . Day after day they pour forth speech" (vv. 1-2, NIV). We cannot learn the plan of redemption—how God sent Jesus in grace to rescue sinners—by studying the natural world; but we can certainly learn about His power, wisdom, and kindness. We can observe the corresponding orders between the patterns in the sky and those in the sea and draw conclusions relevant to our daily Christian experiences. We can add wonder to curiosity and praise to wonder.

I live near Lake Michigan and enjoy driving along the shore or sitting with my children on the beach watching sailboats. I enjoy the sights because of their beauty and sublimity and am compelled to say, whether conscious of the specifics or not, that I learn more about my Lord with each glance. Why else, after all, do poets ponder the sea or the sky or the mountains or an evening storm? The English poet William Wordsworth wrote:

> And I have felt
> A presence that disturbs me with the joy
> Of elevated thoughts; a sense sublime
> Of something far more deeply interfused,
> Whose dwelling is the light of setting suns,
> And the round ocean and the living air,
> And the blue sky, and in the mind of man.

Only a hardened spirit prevents us from recognizing each day the wonders of God's masterpieces all around us.

Science studied apart from Christ misses what is most essential. Likewise, to study human history or literature and the arts apart from the concepts of depravity and redemption or providence and judgment, those issues most central to our ongoing relationship with God, leaves the study without an essential coherence. How can we observe and examine the fruits of a single human life, let alone large sweeps of human history or major themes and motifs in literature, without those larger principles that most define what makes human beings unique, principles taught so plainly in Scripture?

To talk about this created world and the products of the women and men who people it without constant reference to that magnificent Creator, immanent in all His works (see Colossians 1), breeds arrogance and sophistry, not surprisingly the two primary symptoms of the disease suffered by most modern intellectuals. Such a godless approach when filtered down to the average person through our schooling and through the media causes those who lack faith to be hardened in the delusion that God is not relevant to their lives. The result for the average Christian is a compartmentalization of beliefs.

Many American Christians in this present day are not quite sure how to apply their religious beliefs to the details of their daily lives, having not been taught well how to do so, and thus they compartmentalize religious issues over here and "non-religious activity" over there.

Recently a close friend asked me to help repair some weak spots in his attic floor by replacing several boards and securing others. He was gone while I did the work, but a young man who roomed in his house helped me since the repairs were nearest his quarters. This fellow, a very fine young man from a Christian home who attends a nearby university, insisted on playing some CDs from his collection while we worked.

Now the necessity for music defied any logic, because our conversation was interesting. He told me a little about his parents and a mission trip to Chile he had recently taken. I told him about my teaching and my family. Yet, that peculiar habit that drives us modern Americans to play music indiscriminately to accompany everything we do from court our loves to buy our groceries to wash our dishes insisted that the CDs play on. And so we were "entertained" while we worked; the physical exertion of sawing, chiseling, and nailing floor boards was not enough. The presence of the music at the very least hinted that our companionship was dull in that we needed loud distractions to divert attention from each other. And, as one might anticipate, the words of the songs had little bearing on our experiences at the moment and in fact were at times downright embarrassing. One song said something like, "I want you all night long, baby, any way you want to do it to me." Now step back and think about two Christian men whacking nails side by side with those lyrics wafting overhead.

That is a kind of schizophrenia. We accept as normal these glaring gaps between our professed beliefs regarding our God, His world, and our duties in it on the one hand, and many of the practical details of our lives on the other. We may be pretty good in "designated Christian" activities like going to church or Bible class or on a retreat or missions trip, but we are often just awful at doing carpentry or washing dishes or driving our cars or loving our husbands or wives or children—or watching movies.

Left with no solid principles that apply to a subject like film, we are left with ineffective rules— like "I won't allow my young kids to see a PG film, but all Disney films are fine."

But are all Disney films fine? Have Christian parents watched all of *The Little Mermaid* or *Aladdin* or *Pocahontas* and given thought to the messages of these films? One suggests that a sixteen-year-old should be defiant of her father and pursue the person most incompatible with her. One implies that all first dates should end in a kiss. One distorts American history beyond recognition in an age when students need prompting to name the man who discovered America.

No, all Disney films are not fine. And, conversely, some films with sexual content and violence need those components to make important and truthful statements.

One of the best films of the last two decades is a Canadian production directed by Bruce Beresford, entitled *Black Robe* (1991). It contains several scenes of graphic violence and three scenes displaying sexual activity; yet it is one of the most provocative films ever made about the challenges of Christian missionary work. The story is based on a novel drawn from the diary of Noel Chabanel, a martyred seventeenth-century French Jesuit priest who gave his life to bring Christianity to Indians in Canada.

I showed this film in a course in a Christian college once and received an angry letter from a female student who said I had corrupted the innocence of her mind by having her see a film with sexuality that was not "biblical." The irony was that she admitted to having willingly seen two gems of "innocence" and purity, *Pretty Woman* and *Flashdance*.

The temptation is to think that the student didn't like the sexuality in *Black Robe* because it involved American Indians in a smoky teepee rather than Julia Roberts in a glittering American hotel room, but upon reflection a better conclusion is that in the minds of many like this girl, *Pretty Woman* and *Flashdance* are just "entertaining and fun," while *Black Robe* is thoughtful and serious. The rules that apply to the one don't fit the other. This is compartmentalization of the worst kind: My Christian ethics don't need to apply when we are in the realm of "entertainment," but they do need to apply when we are in a serious, even religious, context.

This issue reminds me of a conversation I once had with a pastor from a denomination that need not be named, during which this pastor admitted to taking part in all kinds of hazing activities while in seminary, as well as other behaviors that the apostle Paul would have termed "lawless." He said that it is hard sometimes to face his fellow students, now seminary professors and pastors, given the way they all collectively "sowed their wild oats" when in school. Yet, he commented in a resigned manner that most of his old pals now seem able to block successfully that part of their past from memory. More compartmentalization, more schizophrenia.

Frankly, I am greatly concerned that the American church is already more driven by our culture than by our Christianity. Perhaps this little book will help change that at least in this one area. Our goal is to provoke. Both my collaborator on this project, Christian film reviewer Vernon Edwin Neal, and I hope to offer believers a way to start thinking about films on a deeper level, and in doing so we want to break through some of the apathy and guarded ignorance that has left a great number of our own friends and acquaintances in the Church unwilling to examine their recreational habits seriously.

This book will not answer every question about particular films, and it will certainly not list the films a believer *ought to* watch and those one *ought not*. We will, however, offer principles that might stimulate distinctively Christian thought about the movies, and we will suggest some films that might be conducive to discussion with family and friends.

The best that could happen as a result of our efforts is that many readers will be driven back to Scripture for guidance. After all, a book may provide a few tools and a context for discussion, but God alone provides wisdom.

And it is wisdom that we Christians most need.

Peter Fraser

CHAPTER ONE

A Christian Approach to Film

❦

One problem we seem to have in the modern American church is an inability to accept the world as it exists. We prefer tidier stories with cleaner resolutions and air-brushed images of ourselves rather than the harsh snapshots that catch us as we are, blood of Jesus or no blood of Jesus.

As I begin this chapter, I want very much to offer something safe—five easy-to-read sections on how to choose a video for children, a jeremiad on the depraved art of postmodern western culture, a list of gentle family classics. After all, it is much easier to encourage people to go see *Forrest Gump* than it is to explain why *Body Heat* is one of the better films of recent years. Yet to suggest that *Forrest Gump* is more worth seeing than *Body Heat*, in my mind, would be a kind of lie. *Forrest Gump* may be sweeter and more upbeat, but, all things considered, it isn't better. It isn't even more moral. But, indeed, to explain this opinion is not easy, and so the temptation is to be cowardly and point friends to the Disney shelf.

Once I led a seminar on the subject of Christianity and film in a church, trying my hardest to convey in a couple of short hours, with film clips, what particular issues Christians should consider when going out to a movie or renting a video. Little did I know at the time that it would take an entire book, this one, to work out those details. After my presentation, which included a generous question-and-answer session, as I was gathering up my materials for the long ride home, a woman came up to me and asked the inevitable, "So what are your five favorite films?"

I found I couldn't tell her. So rather than answering her question, I named instead several very good films that address specifically Christian issues head-on—*The Mission, Chariots of Fire, On the Waterfront, Diary of a Country Priest,* and *Tender Mercies.* This list was so much easier to defend than the actual list of my personal favorites, which probably would have led to a long and awkward conversation—films like *Brief Encounter, To Kill a Mockingbird, Swing Time, Babette's Feast,* and even *Uncle Buck.*

I'm not sure I can explain the real list even now, and the past few years have expanded it, although I could make a good case for the quality of each of those films. They just don't all fit a neat discussion of Christianity and the movies.

Yet, the time is at hand for Christians to engage our movie-made culture courageously, and this means we have to struggle with tough issues and tell the truth. Recall that after the Israelites were rebuked and judged for not eliminating the remnant Canaanites in the Promised Land (a laborious task, no doubt), the judgment of the Lord was to allow the Canaanites to survive and prosper and thus be a thorn continuously poking the side of Israel. In the New Testament, believers are told, similarly, to take every thought captive to Christ, do all things to God's glory, overcome the world. When we stand back from engaging the world, in this case the world of film, and instead allow ourselves to be treated like village idiots, we can hardly expect God to be pleased.

We need to face some hard disciplines. The good fight of faith in modern American culture demands that if you are a parent, you ought to watch the films your children are watching and talk about them, and not in a condescending way. It is neglect when our overfilled schedules lead us to use the local video store as a baby-sitting enterprise. Long ago Marie Wynn called television the "plug-in drug" that modern parents give their kids to keep them temporarily docile. The drug has even more potency and worse possible side effects when it plays the elaborately constructed products of Hollywood. Parents must get serious about what their children watch, if indeed they want to train them up in the way they should go.

If you are a teacher, you ought to be using film as a point of contact for those under your charge. More students are familiar with *Schindler's List* than are familiar with *Macbeth*. Some of us still kick against this reality because we love good literature. But why not cross-reference Spielberg instead of Shakespeare to drive home a point? Shakespeare can no longer complain. Crowds at the new Globe in London will not dwindle. And our students might respond better after the point of contact has been established.

Pastors should likewise take note. Hudson Taylor, D. L. Moody, David Brainerd, Amy Carmichael, and Martin Luther will not be forgotten if pastors do not refer to one of them this month. The average congregant has not recently picked up Charles Hodge's *Systematic Theology* or *The Memoirs and Remains of Robert Murray McCheyne* or Metzger's *The Text of the New Testament* or Luther's commentary on Romans. Yet the chances are that about half the people sitting in pews this Sunday will see *It's a Wonderful Life* this Christmas as well as the last five Academy Award nominees for Best Picture. We certainly should never give up the good fight of educating congregations in the best Christian thought, but we need to take care that in attempting to do so we do not start speaking primarily in theological Latin.

When Paul addressed the Athenians gathered at Mars Hill, he did not quote rabbinical teaching. He quoted Greek poets. Likewise he quoted from Greek dramatists, the filmmakers of his day, so to speak, in his epistles. He became a Jew to the Jews and a Greek to the Greeks, "so that by all possible means I might save some" (1 Corinthians 9:22, NIV).

For too long we Christians have feared the corrosive influence of film and so avoided approaching it thoughtfully. We need to shift to the offensive and intentionally discuss film as a way to illustrate and apply the truth. And we need to appreciate film for its artistry and praise our Creator who gives such gifts to men. It may be useful to recall that Jesus never reduced life to simple platitudes, and He never chose the safe, sanitized road. He embraced each person uniquely, and He got his sandals dirty. If films had existed in first-century Israel, it just might be that His tastes would have surprised people. His tastes in people seemed to surprise people, after all.

Beyond the pulpit, classroom, and home, we should also create new contexts for addressing film. The Christian community ought to promote seminars on film. Christian colleges should not only ensure that film be taught as a literary discipline in their individual programs, but promising students ought to be encouraged to pursue graduate studies in film as a ministry to the church. Congregations should encourage small-group get-togethers during which friends can watch and talk about interesting films.

The good news is that the number of Christians who have taken a more thoughtful look at film has increased in the past couple of decades, as evidenced by some of the books on film that have started to appear in Christian bookstores. Furthermore, film classes have grown in popularity on secular college campuses over the past three decades, despite the stuffiness and political correctness of the academic film community, and this growth has spilled onto Christian colleges, where film classes and discussion groups have become more and more common—a dramatic change from the days when many Christian young people signed a pledge not to watch any movies.

Paradoxically, while we engage in this head-on confrontation with what one scholar, Robert Sklar, has called "our movie-made culture," we should all follow Job's lead (cf. 31:1) and make a covenant with ourselves and God to practice the fine art of self-discipline. In a consumer society like our own in which "goods" are plentiful and so easily accessible, we need to be discriminating.

In 1 Corinthians 10 Paul reminds us that all things are lawful but not all things edify. Now, the average person does not go to a theater to be edified. He goes for cheap entertainment. He sees whatever is playing that looks "pretty good"—translated, that won't prove dull. Christians, on the other hand, should always have in mind what is edifying. Paul tells us in Philippians to think on the good, the true, the noble. But we tend to follow the shepherding of our all-pervasive pop culture and watch movies the way Americans eat—too much and with little thought of the art. We absorb indiscriminately and consequently begin to fill out like everyone else.

The opposite should be true. In an age of drunkenness, Christians ought to be models of sobriety. In an age of crudeness, Christians ought to be models of purity. In an age of divorce, Christians ought to be models of faithfulness. And in an age of movie-gluttony, Christians ought to practice selectivity and restraint. This is no contradiction of the previous point about educating ourselves. What I am advocating here is responsibility. We can be savvy about film without having seen *Halloween 8* or the latest macho-superhero thriller.

If you have the misfortune of visiting an allergist and she or he detects a food allergy, you may find yourself placed on a highly restrictive diet. Your initial food allowance will include only the most bland of staples; then your doctor will slowly allow you to reintroduce other foods one by one, monitoring your reaction to each new food. This is an imperfect analogy, but it conveys the point that Christians should not treat films like Easter jelly beans. Images and ideas stay in the system much too long and can produce a wide range of effects.

If there is no coherence to the way we watch film, if the very notion of a Christian approach to film is puzzling, then it may be prudent to pull away from the screen entirely to allow ourselves time to regroup.

There is really no good excuse for a shoddy Christian life. There are numerous books on the market that discuss film, and not just chatty books about celebrities. There are available good scholarly books written in plain English that provide histories of narrative film, introductions to film analysis, and discussions of the nature of popular film styles and genres. With the development of the Internet, many such resources are also available online (if we can wade through the muck of pornographic and ill-informed sites to access the good ones). We can also do some digging at home or in our local library. Public and educational television upon occasion produces documentaries about film that are usually quite insightful, such as the *American Cinema* series produced in the early nineties by the Annenberg School. And many colleges, unfortunately more secular than Christian, offer introductory courses in film that are relatively inexpensive to take for credit or audit. In Romans 13 Paul tells us to awake from our slumber because our salvation comes nearer each day. Certainly his admonition fits our present context.

Before launching into some particulars that may provide some help for Christians who want a thoughtful approach to film, let me briefly describe and comment upon the three ways that Christians have tended historically to respond to film. The three often constitute attitudes even more than they do theories, but I will explain them as if they were completely thought out.

The first is the notion that for Christians to use films for the work of Christ, *they* must make those films. The second is the related idea that the connection between the Christian faith and a particular film has to do with the subject matter of the film. The third is the idea that Christianity addresses film only if a viewer can find Christian symbols and types. The first two approaches indicate typical popular conceptions regarding the kinds of film that Christians should support. The third is what I consider to be the primary academic fallacy of Christians who approach film as a form of scholarship.

Over the past thirty years an increasing number of films have been produced by evangelical and fundamentalist Christian groups like World Wide Pictures (the Billy Graham Association), Ken Anderson Films, and Moody Films. Some of the more successful early endeavors were *The Hiding Place* (1975), *The Cross and the Switchblade* (1972), and *Jesus of Nazareth* (1975). A more recent title that might be more familiar is *The Spitfire Grill* (1996), a film sponsored by a Catholic organization, The Sacred Heart League; the movie was then sold to an independent distributor, Castle Rock Films.

These films are generally low-budget productions with moderate to poor artistic quality, the limited resources and talent working against the overall aesthetic conception. The films tend to be sermonic, with many ending outright with a gospel message.

In *The Spitfire Grill*, for example, a young woman, Percy Talbott, recently released from eight years in prison, comes to a small town in Maine for a new start. The town's name is, significantly, Gilead. She goes to work at the town grill, the Spitfire Grill, owned by a crotchety older woman with a painful past, Hannah Ferguson. Hannah has been trying to sell the grill for years, and Percy suggests she raffle it off, an unusual scheme that nonetheless proves successful. The townspeople, especially Hannah's nephew Nahum, grow suspicious of Percy, but she succeeds eventually in winning over Hannah, Nahum's wife Shelby, and a mysterious stranger who lurks in the woods, who predictably turns out to be Hannah's son, unbalanced since returning from the war.

Before the film is over, everyone around Percy is redeemed by her various actions, especially after Percy . . . I will stop here in case you see the film.

Reviews of *The Spitfire Grill* were mostly polarized. On one side were the usual critics who pretty much agreed that the film, in the words of Renshaw, "slaps, kicks, pinches, and pleads" for tears. On the other hand were the Christian critics who, in the words of Dale Mason, thought the film "an excellent choice with several refreshing Christian overtones." The conclusion to draw from this is that Christians who want to see movies about Christianity loved the film, whereas most people who simply wanted to see a good film found it heavy-handed and implausible. That is to say, they thought the film lied. Life isn't this tidy. Personally, I thought the film would be a great choice for my children, up to a certain age. It may be conceivable that people could behave this way somewhere and that events could unfold in this fashion. But overall the film is indeed syrupy and preachy.

Nonetheless, for some fundamentalist Christians, films like *The Spitfire Grill* are a better kind of film. The assumption is that because they have been conceived and produced by Christians, and because they are orthodox and didactic, they honor God. According to the same logic, of course, all mainstream films, which are purely commercial enterprises, are profane.

I do not blame Christians who feel this way. At least half of the films my wife and I see prove somewhat offensive either because of the juvenile or salacious content or because of the way they stereotype Christians. The church needs to influence film production as the church has done throughout the centuries for other arts. In time, great films will come from the church. *The Spitfire Grill*, despite its weaknesses, may indeed be a step in the right direction, and unquestionably many Christian-made films have been used of God—think of the *Jesus* film. The point here is that films made by Christians or sponsored by Christians may still be poor films; in fact, the majority of them, at the date of this writing, are. Throughout history, Christians have produced much of the world's great art and provided some of the most insightful criticism of classic and contemporary art. We have a long way to go to meet these past standards in the medium of film.

The tendency to prioritize films made by Christians also creates one rather large problem. Which branches of the church will be allowed to have the label *Christian*? Will evangelicals, for example, allow Catholics to be included? If so, an enormous number of films will suddenly fall under the label of Christian film, including Francis Ford Coppola's *The Godfather* and *Apocalypse Now*, Brian De Palma's *Carrie* and *Dressed to Kill*, Alfred Hitchcock's *Psycho*, and even Martin Scorsese's *The Last Temptation of Christ*. If Catholic productions are excluded, there are new problems. What do you do with manifestly brilliant films by Catholics such as Frank Borzage's thorough Christianization of the Hemingway story *A Farewell to Arms* or the French director Robert Bresson's pious devotional films on

Christian topics? To dismiss such films would dismiss indis-
putable works of genius, landmarks in the evolution of film
style, and, more importantly, works that are laced with large
Christian intentions. In addition, as soon as we begin to favor
one Christian expression over another—Lutheran versus
Catholic, Anglican, Presbyterian, or Baptist—we open the door
for an odd variety of artistic bias.

It is obvious from this that a Christian attempting a serious
approach to film must step beyond simply looking for films
made by Christians. Yet, the Christian public may always tend
to prioritize films with some sort of overt Christian label, if only
because it is easier to understand how to respond to them.

The second way that Christians tend to approach film is to
prioritize those that have Christian subjects—like *A Man for All
Seasons* about Thomas More, *Romero* about the courageous El
Salvadoran archbishop, and *Shadowlands* about C. S. Lewis.
This is one reason for the past success of biblical spectaculars,
historically one of Hollywood's most successful film genres. Six
of the top ten money-making films in the 1950s were biblical
spectaculars, and although the genre has faded in the last few
decades, the biblical film remains a favorite during holiday seasons. *The Robe* (1953), *Ben Hur* (1959), and *King of Kings*
(1961) are three of the most frequently seen films of all time.
Biblical films and religious epics in general are also frequently
remade. The epic *Quo Vadis?* (1951), for example, has been
filmed three times, as has *Ben Hur*. But it is not only the purely
biblical story that has maintained enormous popularity in
America. Films about religious people and religious events have
had similar success. *Boys' Town* (1938), *The Song of Bernadette*
(1943), *Going My Way* (1944), *The Bells of St. Mary's* (1945),
and, more recently, *Chariots of Fire* (1981) have all become cult
films for many American Christians.

The unique success of films about religious subjects must be explained beyond the inherent quality of these films or their inherent piety. Only one or two of these productions, perhaps *Ben Hur* and *Chariots of Fire*, are commonly recognized as examples of great filmmaking. Some biblical epics have been ranked among the worst films ever made. *The Bible* (1966) and *The Greatest Story Ever Told* (1965) are two well-acknowledged examples. Similarly, the religious sentiments of the majority of these films are highly suspect. Many of the Jesus films demolish the integrity of the Lord's words. Almost all of the biblical films introduce fictional characters and plot devices in an attempt to add continuity and relevance to the biblical accounts. In *King of Kings* Barabbas is given a complete history that is used as a contrast to the life of Christ. In *The Ten Commandments*, an Egyptian maid in Pharaoh's court, who loves Moses, pleads with him not to defy Pharaoh in a decidedly womanish way. In the non-biblical religious films, like *Chariots of Fire*, Christian principles are linked with patriotic and nationalistic sentiments; the success of the Christian is tied in with the virtue of the political ideal.

The popularity of these "Christian" films is not a function of quality or religious integrity so much as it is a suggestion of the power of the popular belief that films about religious figures (like films made by Christians) are somehow more worth watching. The mere reference to Christian subjects is considered a good thing, regardless of how this reference is developed.

I vividly recall seeing the original Indiana Jones film with a youth group and a subsequent conversation during which several of my Christian friends argued that it was a good thing to have a film like *Raiders of the Lost Ark* make people aware of the ark of the covenant and the Jewish faith. Puzzle over this one awhile.

Christians should not have a cheap and uninformed attitude

toward a film's overall message. Because a film company gestures toward a Christian community, we should not all bow down in thanksgiving. What a gross distortion it is to have the secular filmmaking industry throwing offerings toward the church to help her deliver her message. A poor film about gospel truth may be more dangerous than a film that espouses the death of God. Christians may watch religious films and glean out blessings from them as they are reminded of what the Scriptures actually record, but religious films are not a better kind of film just because they quote religious material.

A recent example of this was the attention given the film *The Matrix* by many evangelicals who noted overt Christian references throughout the film, like the name of a sanctuary for refugees being "Zion." What was often overlooked in the discussion was the fact that the film also celebrates "beautiful violence" and magazine-cover virtue. (Pretty much the bottom line for *Raiders of the Lost Ark* too, although *Raiders* is a far superior film.) For every Christian who left the theater mulling over the philosophic and religious hints in the film, ten other viewers left the theater either talking about the special effects or how "hot" Keanu Reaves and Carrie Ann Moss looked.

On to the third way that Christians have tried to apply their faith to film: The majority of scholarly articles about film written by Christians in the Academy have applied structural methods to certain films in an attempt to extract biblical themes and symbols. Structuralism is a method of literary and film criticism in which a text is treated as a closed system of meaning waiting to be decoded. The George Lucas *Star Wars* series and Stephen Spielberg's *E.T.* have been discussed in journals by Christian structuralists as Christian allegories. In *Star Wars* (1977), Luke Skywalker has been said to resemble either David (or Christ) preparing for his position as king. The Force is the power of the

Holy Spirit. Darth Vader is the fallen angel Lucifer. The battles are for the souls of mankind. In *E.T.* (1980), the extraterrestrial is Christ, come down to earth to teach mankind a higher law. He hides in a shed (a manger) and is discovered and cared for by children (the disciples), persecuted by adult authorities, killed, and then raised from the dead. His ascension is witnessed by a newly formed community of believers.

The approach taken with these films is not new. A famous 1952 western, Fred Zinnemann's *High Noon*, has received similar treatment, as have a host of other films that contain biblical motifs and symbols. The fact is that a large number of films are saturated with Christian allusions that can be picked out and hung on some logical clothesline. The simplest explanation for this is cultural: The mainstream American public has retained the outer structures of Christianity. Another explanation is that a striking number of important Hollywood filmmakers were brought up in religious families, most often Catholic: Leo McCarey, Fritz Lang, Frank Borzage, John Ford, Alfred Hitchcock, Francis Ford Coppola, Paul Schrader, Martin Scorsese, etc. Christian scholars have no difficulty tracing traditional Christian motifs in Hollywood films, and, I might suggest, the project is a safe one—satisfying to the scholar and harmless to the film industry.

The flaw in this structural approach toward Christianity in film is that it often skirts the more significant questions regarding what an individual film is saying. In other words, the Christian symbols found in films are rarely interpreted in the light of their specific context. It is thought by some writers to be enough to merely point them out. The significant question for the Christian, however, should be, "What does the symbol—the cross, or the motif of light versus darkness—mean *here*?" Instead of asking that, scholars merely praise the appearance of the symbol, as if its meaning is inviolate. This practice would lead to a complete misreading of a film like *The Matrix* in which Christian symbols abound in a sci-fi story more akin to Frank Herbert's *Dune* than to the Bible.

These, then, are the three ways in which Christians have tried to apply issues of faith to film. What characterizes all three is reductivism. Whether you say we should pay attention to films made by Christians, films about Christians, or films heavy in traditional Christian symbols, you are ultimately saying that Christians primarily care about the superficial characteristics of art. We don't care about the artfulness of art, nor its honesty. If we can simply slap a label on a film based on its most obvious characteristics, we do not need to take the time to understand the uniqueness of that film and to examine its particular strengths and weaknesses. These are the safe methods, however, and thus practiced frequently.

Christians need to show more courage and insight. We must tackle both the important issues of film quality and the issue of a film's overall meaning and significance. We must come up with a critical strategy that has enough meat and bones to stand up beside the politically charged interpretive strategies that are now current in the university. After all, if we cannot hold our own against proponents of Marxist, feminist, and homosexual/lesbian theories, we are in dire straits. So, what should a Christian look for when watching a film?

Our first concern should be *cinematic and dramatic excellence*. Regardless of the message of the individual film, Christians ought to be the first to recognize and praise a film's artistry. All beauty reflects God's beauty, whether it is understood to be from the Creator or not. Shoddiness and mass-produced hack art should offend us on some level, regardless of who produces it or what it is about. To soak in mediocrity is not exactly what one would call "following the high call of Christ." Paul tells us to think on the "excellent" (Philippians 4:8, NIV), not the contrived. The Scriptures teach that human endeavor should replicate God's own endeavors and praise Him. God pronounced His work "good."

What this means practically is that we should feel an obligation to learn what "good" filmmaking is. Beyond the suggestions offered above and the others yet to come, one simple way to learn this is by studying classic films. You don't become a connoisseur of fine food by eating at McDonald's.

In this regard a list of excellent films, like the one generated by the American Film Institute, or notices about films that have received awards—Golden Globe, Academy, Cannes, Sundance Festival—have their place. A useful exercise is to try to learn what people who study film or create film see in the "good" films.

A film has many component parts, such as cinematography, sound, editing, acting, costume and stage design, story. One quality of all great art is its ability to blend all its parts in a way that captivates and engages the imaginations and feelings of a large number of people. The poet Emily Dickinson once suggested that a writer knows she has created a good poem when it feels like the top of her head comes off. The experience should be the same for the reader, or viewer in this case. Notice how some people remain seated during the credits of a film. Many of them are trying to catch their breath, so to speak. After Roberto Benigni's *Life Is Beautiful* played at our local theater, very few people wanted to leave their seats. I recall having a similar powerful response to Martin Scorsese's *Age of Innocence*. Plato believed that poets were possessed by the Muses because of the power inherent in their art. A great film is felt deeply—it has acting that makes your mouth drop; it leaves stirring images. When it ends, be it tragic or comic, you are somewhat sad.

Film likewise weaves together a variety of separate arts—storytelling, photography, theater, music, sometimes poetry and painting. A great film is, indeed, a thing to be reckoned with. It is a nearly miraculous human production, a simulation of life played out through multiple artistic media. The appearance of a beautifully made film, even one that comes from someone far from the church, ought to be celebrated by Christians. A great film carries with it the story of our God who so loved man whom He had created that He shared with him the ability to produce from dust a flower. Art is our own invention of the flower. The creation of an artful film is a wonderful thing.

The second criterion for the interpretation and evaluation of films by the Christian should be *integrity*. By this I mean the resonance of a film—a film's ability to capture truths and convey them. This is a slippery category; it sounds like I am creating it out of a bias toward realistic films or didactic films, but I have no such bias. Film integrity is as much an evaluative approach to fantasy or animated film as it is to drama. It refers to the filmmaker's statements about the world, not the language chosen to clothe those statements.

Think of great literature. No reader would claim that Cervantes's *Don Quixote* records life as lived; yet all readers respond to the character of the romantic knight who thinks La Mancha is the home of fighting heroes and needy damsels. We may have never met a deranged man who wore armor, but we have all met Don Quixote—we meet him when we look in the mirror. The truth of *Don Quixote* is so powerful that the English language has a word—*quixotic*—to describe that dreamy hero in us all.

Film, as is true of all art forms, should create or reflect a world that rings true, a world fallen and in need of grace, a world in which the only hope for resolution and individual salvation *is* the Gospel. A film can be comic or satirical and still make a direct statement about man and the world. Similarly and more directly to the point, a film does not need to be overtly Christian or heavily symbolic to have a resonance for the Christian. What it needs is truth. Characters must be representatives of fallen humanity, and events must be as they are in experience, marred and groaning as the earth groans for salvation. A director of any faith can make such a film about any subject using any dramatic strategy, for any man who tells the truth will testify to the experience of the whole of suffering, fallen humanity.

My favorite film is a little British gem made by David Lean in 1945, called *Brief Encounter*. The story is of two married people who meet at a train station and then meet again by chance later in the same day, and then in time fall accidentally in love. The woman, from whose point of view the story is told, suffers much in the unfolding of the relationship, because she is already happily married to a good, if a bit dull, man, and they have two children. I will not reveal too much about the story, since it may spoil it for some, but it may be permissible to mention that the conflict leads to a real choice between a genuine yet sinful passion and the moral right—and the choice is presented as difficult.

The artistry of *Brief Encounter* has been widely recognized. It may be the most visually poetic film ever made. The problem for Christians would be in the subject matter; after all, it is a film about adultery. But it is a film that presents adultery truthfully; that is, the characters face a situation that is quite plausible, and they react to it quite plausibly. Whether or not we approve of the choices they make is another matter altogether. The concern here is for the story's integrity, proof of which can be found not only in our own experience in this world, but in the numerous other great works of literature that present a similar story in a similar way—Tolstoy's *Anna Karenina*, Flaubert's *Madame Bovary*, Chekhov's "The Lady with the Dog," Kate Chopin's *The*

Awakening, to name a few. That adultery is wrong and that we wished it would never happen and that we hope and pray that we never are tempted in that way is beside the point. The point is that it does happen, even to "good" people, made in God's own image to love and worship Him, and they suffer as a result.

At issue is how the subject is presented and to what purpose. *Brief Encounter* begs us to feel compassion for human beings in a broken world who want to be happy, but do not have the strength on their own to accomplish that. I have found in my teaching career both in a large state university and at two Christian colleges that it is far more effective for me to discuss the Gospel and my personal faith in the context of a work of art like *Brief Encounter* than it is in the context of a work that is explicitly Christian. Everyone listens and is moved in the former discussion. In the latter, only the choir hears.

This brings to mind a recent experience in a Christian college in which I was discussing with a group of students the American Puritan poet Anne Bradstreet, whose poetry is standard reading in survey courses but nowhere else. I asked the class what they thought the responsibility of a Christian writer like Bradstreet ought to be. Several hands went up. One student suggested that Christian writers should choose subjects that are edifying. Another suggested that Christian poets should write about the Gospel. Another spoke about the language that the poet should use. Finally, after some discussion, a student in the corner of the room, chewing thoughtfully on a toothpick, raised his hand and said, "A Christian poet should do everything possible to keep from being called a hypocrite." It was a perfect response, although few of the other students caught the subtle implications.

Since our Lord is "the truth," we should be people of the truth who do not need to mask the realities of human existence. Jesus became flesh to save sinners, which we are. We groan and suffer and wait for grace. The earth groans for redemption, because it has suffered the curse of the Fall too. The Gospel declares that God has seen us in our sin and misery and loves us. We are saved by grace, not by our own goodness. True Christian art celebrates grace, and to do so it will tell the truth.

A film is made by people, individuals working together, and it needs to be evaluated as the collective speech of a group of people, sinful people hopeless apart from grace. Is it truth or does it lie? Here is a crucial artistic question. We Christians need to recognize that we alone stand in a place where that question might be answered with confidence.

Celia Johnson plays an ordinary woman caught between darkness and light in David Lean's masterpiece *Brief Encounter* (1945).

CHAPTER TWO

LEARNING THE LANGUAGE

☙

There is little space in this book to go into all the detailed intricacies of how films are made. The production side of film has its own scholarly turf, and whereas anecdotes are often passed from the producers of films to the critics like us, and vice versa, the how-tos of making movies and the wherebys of interpreting them are best discussed separately. The intent here is to stay on the side of interpretation and offer some basic principles that help create a frame for discussing the quality and meaningfulness of a particular movie.

The first of these principles is that films can appear deceptively simple but are usually rather complex in design. In fact, film by its very nature is a grand deception. When watching a film, we think we are watching moving images, but in actuality the only thing that moves in the motion picture is the celluloid through the projector. Films are a string of still photographs that, when passed rapidly before our eyes at speeds from sixteen to twenty-four frames per second, appear to move because of two optical illusions—persistence of vision and the phi phenomenon. Persistence of vision is the optical phenomenon whereby images are held in our perception slightly longer than they actually appear before us. The phi phenomenon is the optical effect that causes fan blades and automobile tires to appear as a solid image when spinning rapidly.

The appearance of motion is only the beginning deception, of course. When we watch a film, we are led to think we are watching action occurring in sequence, when in reality most films are shot out of sequence, only to be rearranged on the editing table. Likewise, we think we are hearing the sound of actors and the environment around them as they perform, whereas film sounds rarely match the actual sound of the acted scene; film editors have pulled all of those sounds out and altered or replaced them, including the dialogue. These examples are only the most obvious. The great irony of the filmmaker's art is that whereas the final product appears more natural and lifelike than any other form that artists can produce, it is perhaps the most contrived and illusory.

Years ago when I was a graduate student in English at the University of Illinois at Chicago, I changed my emphasis from American literature to film and popular culture. I had at the time the mistaken notion that what I had learned studying literary texts would make it easy to understand film texts. It wasn't until I floundered through a semester's work that I realized that the language of film is much different than the language of literature.

Many people suffer this same misconception. Because of the narrative qualities of many films, they tend to speak about films in the same way they speak about novels and short stories, making exclusive reference to themes and symbols and character motivation and setting—all things related to plot. Consider the typical response of a person watching a film based on their favorite novel. The person who has read and enjoyed the novel invariably points out where the filmmaker has altered the story and thus "ruined it" in some way, as if film, the lesser art by implication, is supposed merely to dramatize existing stories. The truth, of course, is that a film cannot tell a story in the same way a novel does. Films follow different aesthetic rules.

No matter what a novel is about, how well it is written or poorly, what the length or what the author's style, the novel communicates exclusively through printed words. When we determine a novel's theme, we analyze the systematic use of those words and how they lead to the creation of character, setting, plot, conflict, and resolution.

Although we approach film in a similar way, looking for a unified language that builds systematic structures of coherent expression, we have to recognize that the language of film is not principally built upon words. Films speak primarily through images and sounds.

In fact, the literal story of the film, the part that could be written down as a sequence of events, may be the least interesting part. Think, for example, about musicals. Very few people watch Fred Astaire and Ginger Rogers films like *Top Hat* or *Swing Time* with an eye to the details of the story. Rather, the story provides a thin justification for the song and dance numbers that make the films delightful and meaningful.

Musicals are just one easy example. The same might be said of many action films or horror films or suspense thrillers. A classic example can be found in one of the more notable films that starred Humphrey Bogart and Lauren Bacall in the 1940s, *The Big Sleep*. This hard-boiled detective mystery is so atmospheric and heavy with memorable performances that an entire murder goes unexplained in the course of the action, and very few viewers ever notice. The story is far less significant than the visual components of the film. A more recent example of the same phenomenon can be found in the movie *Seven*, in which the dark atmosphere created visually on the screen overpowers every other element in the film and leaves the final impression.

Film, unlike written literature, is by nature a composite art form. As mentioned earlier, it can incorporate a range of artistic modalities—dance, theater, painting, poetry, and song. As with architecture, a group of technicians with wide-ranging skills work together under one director to create the final product. The author is much more a supervisor of others in the film industry than he is the lonely poet in the drafty garret. This artistic complexity, I believe, accounts for the unique appeal and power that films can have.

The most frightening moment in the 1975 film *Jaws*, a film that most Americans have seen at least once, occurs midway through the action when the shark first rises with gaping jaws from the water. Nearly everyone who sees this scene for the first time jumps. Why? From the beginning of the film a certain visual and auditory pattern was set up by director Steven Spielberg. When the shark is in the vicinity, the famous, percussive theme music begins to play in the background. Then we wait several seconds and typically get the shark's point of view as it approaches its victim. We are horrified, yet prepared for the gruesome shark attacks. Since this pattern is repeated three or four times, we assume as viewers that Spielberg has given us a language system that will continue to the end of the film.

Our assumptions, however, get undermined. In the scene of the shark's first full appearance, the Roy Scheider character is tossing bloody fish into the water to lure the shark to the boat, where he and two other men plan to harpoon and kill it. Scheider faces the camera away from the water and yells some comments to the other men, when suddenly without warning, without the musical cue, the shark rises out of the water with its jaws gaping wide. Scheider turns and rises in terror; we do too.

The effect is caused by Spielberg's manipulation of our expectations regarding an established pattern of images and sound. We were led to think, whether consciously or not, that the shark's appearance would always follow the percussive musical cue. This time it did not.

In describing that moment to someone who has not seen the film, you are left at a bit of a loss. To say, "The shark suddenly rises out of the water" may describe that development in the plot, but it hardly captures the essence of what happens in the experience of watching the film. Spielberg's effect is a function of film editing, sound track, and camera point of view, terms that have no precise equivalent in written literature.

This complex nature of film likewise renders it difficult at times to pinpoint what makes certain films succeed as well as they do. Try to explain to someone the power of the final sequences from Francis Ford Coppola's *The Godfather*. As Michael Corleone (Al Pacino) holds his baby and makes his baptismal vows to renounce Satan and train his son up in the ways of the Lord, members of his organization murder the heads of the rival Mafia families. Coppola edits the sequence as a montage with shots of the baptism crosscut with shots of the murders being committed. The power and suggestiveness of the sequence is in the juxtaposed images with their ironic contrasts. To convey this to someone appropriately, you would have to show a video clip. A surface description would not express enough.

Take another example from a film that ought to be familiar to most Christians, the 1981 Academy Award winner *Chariots of Fire*. In the climactic sequence, Eric Liddell (Ian Charleson), a Christian missionary running a dash in the 1924 Olympics, easily defeats the field in the 400-meter race and wins a gold medal for Britain. That is what happens. What we see and hear is profoundly more complex—Liddell's inner thoughts are spoken in a voice-over recalling an earlier scene, the film sequence cuts from real time to slow motion, the camera lens narrows the focal range blurring the background; then the film cuts back to real time, and shots of Liddell are crosscut with reaction shots of his sister and brother in the crowd as well as several British dignitaries and a rival runner. Add to this the introduction of the Vangelis score and several other aspects of visual texture, all in a sequence of less than a half minute, and you have an exceedingly complex and powerful film experience—difficult to explain, yet the essential reason for the film's box office and critical success. The story contributes largely, of course, but the success of *Chariots of Fire* depends on the artistry that makes the story move us.

As Christians who want to speak to our world about or through the art of cinema, we are thus faced with the challenge of learning how this art works. If we fail in this regard, our discussions will rarely get beyond the surface of the topics that films raise. We will be left with a partial understanding and no significant audience beyond the choir.

What follows will be a simple breakdown of the major component parts of a film with some discussion of how each contributes to the whole. As mentioned earlier, more developed discussions of the elements of film can be found in a variety of good texts, some of which we mention later. For now it will suffice to simply introduce the concepts of shot composition, photography, motion, editing, sound, acting, and story.

SHOT COMPOSITION

Since film is basically a string of still images rapidly flashed before our eyes, its power will largely depend on the excellence of those individual images. The cinematographer of a film has as a first concern the quality of the individual photos that his camera creates.

This interesting "iris shot" from Hugh Hudson's *Chariots of Fire* (1981) communicates both the developing romance between two of the main characters and the proud history that surrounds their story.

Hand your young son or daughter a camera and have them take a photograph of you and what will happen? Chances are the photo will only frame half your face, or your legs will be chopped off, or the camera will have captured your expression in the precisely wrong moment. It takes practice to create good photos, and not just technically accurate ones either, but those that capture the spirit of the image as well as the letter.

Put a good film in your VCR and randomly pause it. Each individual composition ought to have interesting elements in it. Some images will certainly stand out more than others—these are the images that will find their way into trailers and promotional packets—but all the images should make some statement.

I had this driven home recently in a film class during which we analyzed Robert Redford's fine 1992 adaptation of Norman MacLean's great short novel *A River Runs Through It*. After watching the film in its entirety as a class, we watched it again, pausing wherever the imagery warranted comment. Needless to say, we could not get far, because one student or another would urge that I pause the film for comment. The very first shot in the film is of an old man's hands engaged in tying a fly to a fishing line. The class spent at least ten minutes discussing why this shot of just the old man's hands was so particularly suitable to what the film was saying as a whole. In this respect, watching a great film is like wandering through an art gallery. The more sophisticated the film visually, the longer you want to stay in the gallery.

Another illustration of this from the classroom would be those occasions when I have shown classes segments of two versions of the same film. Recently I did this, showing first David Lean's 1945 masterpiece *Brief Encounter*, discussed in the previous chapter, and then a segment of a 1984 American remake of that film entitled *Falling in Love*. In the original version you can pause the film in nearly every spot and find something interesting to talk about—the unusual camera position, the shadowy compositions, the manner in which ordinary objects are foregrounded in highly emotional scenes. Watching the remake you find yourself wondering why a scene that had such power in the original comes across so flat here. The individual images are the problem, for they have little of the visual interest of those in David Lean's film. Technical competency simply becomes tedious when juxtaposed with artistry and inspiration. Like a great canvas, there is a luminous quality to a great film. The shots are arranged in ways that intrigue and delight us, even in cases where the subject itself may be unpleasant.

Two of the past summer's (1999) most discussed films illustrate the strange appeal of unpleasant subjects, Stanley Kubrick's last film *Eyes Wide Shut* and the low-budget horror sensation *The Blair Witch Project*. Neither film is family fare, and I would only recommend one or the other to specialized audiences; yet both have noteworthy technical merit. Kubrick's film is a parable about the dangers of pursuing the illusions of sexual temptation, and in it he bombards the viewer with alternately attractive and grotesque images of human sexuality. *Blair Witch* is pure psychological horror with an abundance of dark and disorienting images that linger afterward and trouble the mind. Whether or not these are great films, they have excellent visual qualities. (The issue of film content will be saved for a later discussion.)

PHOTOGRAPHY

One of the more visually striking films of the last few decades was the rousing 1971 adaptation of Joseph Stein's hit play *Fiddler on the Roof*, starring Chaim Topol as Rev Tevye, the good-hearted, hardworking father of a poor Jewish family in Russia. Unlike a Kubrick film or a bit of horror like *Blair Witch*, this is family fare, and the best kind since it is not only a nice story but also a great piece of filmmaking. What most people remember about *Fiddler on the Roof* is the marvelous John Williams scoring of the music of Sheldon Harnick and Jerry Bock, including the favorites "If I Were a Rich Man" and "Sunrise, Sunset." Yet the power of those songs in the film has as much to do with the gorgeous photographic backdrops given them as it does the music. Oswald Morris won an Oscar for this cinematography in fact.

The cinematography of *Fiddler on the Roof* can be best appreciated when shots in the film are viewed in sequences. When two images are juxtaposed in a film, joined in what is known as a cut or dissolved together, the composition of those spliced images must somehow blend into the overall rhythm of the sequence in which they are contained. The main rule for editing together visual sequences is the concept of the graphic match, a technique whereby visual motifs from one image are carried into following images to create continuity. When Topol dances and sings during the heavily rhythmic "If I Were a Rich Man," the images imitate the music's rhythm and texture, and there is a symmetrical quality to the framing of each shot. The cuts occur at the end of musical phrases, and they are definitive and abrupt, fewer in number yet with greater contrast. During "Sunrise, Sunset" the cuts are more fluid, likewise following the liquid rhythms of the music, and the swaying effect of the musical line is imitated visually by a sequence of facial shots taken from alternate sides of the visual plane—you see one face on the left of the screen, then another on the right. Each face is lit with the glow of a candle. Each represents a distinct point of view. Each has its own beauty. And all the shots taken together form a uniform impression.

This is what a good cinematographer can bring to a film—beautiful individual images blended into a beautifully coherent whole. Well-constructed films have visual dynamics that move us as subtly and powerfully as a strong harmonic base to a song or lyric poem. Some of the films that come to mind immediately as testaments to great photography are not surprisingly some of the great films of the twentieth century—*Citizen Kane*, *Sunrise*, *On the Waterfront*, *Wuthering Heights*, and, more recently, *Black Robe* and *Age of Innocence*.

MOTION

Above everything perhaps, moving pictures have to move. The illusion that makes the cinema possible, persistence of vision, whereby we see still photos flashed in rapid sequence as moving, demands in its way that we who watch films are swept through the films. This is a metaphor, of course, but there is sound logic underneath. Film that doesn't move might as well go back to being still photography or theater.

The point is made with a look at some very early films. The earliest filmmakers, Thomas Edison in the United States and Auguste and Louis Lumiere in France, planted their cameras in one spot and recorded whatever happened to be or was placed in front of them—a man sneezing, a train coming into a station, workers leaving a factory. To original audiences who watched these short wonders they were landmark achievements, but to present-day audiences they are quaint and dull. We wonder why nobody thought to move the camera around or edit it together into a story. Filmmakers would, of course, within a decade or two, but even those somewhat later films seem rather stiff compared to the swirling action of the modern cinema. Just as cinema has evolved toward greater visual sophistication as photographic technology has advanced, and just as film has evolved as a sound medium as the technology of sound has evolved, so film has evolved in the direction of greater and greater motion. The modern camera is much more active, editing is more intricate and rhythmic, and sets are more dynamic. Compare a film like *Saving Private Ryan* to any great war film of the past, say Lewis Milestone's *All Quiet on the Western Front* (1930), a classic in its own right, and you can't help but find the older film slightly static in the battle sequences when compared to the Spielberg film. Your eye is drawn to all corners of the screen to follow the action of *Saving Private Ryan*. Bullets seem to be whistling past you as you sit watching. You are placed as a viewer inside the action on the screen and thus are exhilarated or terrified.

As with shot composition, the great directors find a way to involve us in the motion of the film's narrative action. Take a look at the well-known car chase sequence from *The French*

Connection, William Friedkin's Oscar-winning 1971 action film about a detective's attempt to break up a heroin ring. Friedkin puts us inside the car during the chase by photographing just behind the main actor, Gene Hackman. We see what he sees and thus experience the flight of his car from a purely subjective point of view. Our actual vision is limited by the confined space, and yet our sense of the "thrill of the chase" is magnified. Contrast this with any mediocre action film. Go rent an awful exploitation film just for fun, like *Gator Bait II,* and marvel at how dull a chase can be in the hands of a hack director. The thrill is missing in some films that exists in others because one director, and cinematographer and film editor, understands better than the next how to make a moving picture move.

Recently I watched a film for the first time that had been highly recommended to me when first released in 1981, Louis Malle's *My Dinner with Andre.* In it two friends meet over dinner and talk for nearly two hours about their experiences with life and the theater; one is an actor and playwright, the other a director. *My Dinner with Andre* was a highly experimental art film that created a bit of a stir with the university crowd of which I was a part at that time. The conversation between the two, Andre Gregory and Wallace Shawn, is at times engaging and clever as they share theatrical anecdotes and wisdom, although the passing of time has eroded some of the verbal originality. But what is particularly apparent seeing it for the first time nearly twenty years since its release is how dreadfully slow it moves. The actors don't go anywhere, not even up from the table and to the restroom. The camera never breaks from a basic shot/reverse-shot record of the speaker speaking and listener listening. Watching it now produces a kind of cinematic claustrophobia. The conversation might be great, but if I want a record of conversation, I could read a transcript. When I go to see a film, I want to forget that I am sitting in one spot staring forward for two hours.

A film must move us to a different place. It must take us into a room and through it. *Titanic* accomplished this for millions of people. It took us from the most elegant of dining rooms through narrow, water-filled corridors, and finally placed us in the middle of the ocean watching a great ship slowly slide into the water. I think that in twenty years what I will remember most about *Titanic*, beyond its momentary definition of American popular culture, will be the sense of despair I felt during that scene, because somehow I had been moved out of my comfortable seat into those cold waters, watching my friends turn blue, watching all the lights before me go out. That moment was a type of damnation. It was Dante walking through the underworld. Sadly, the entire film couldn't live up to that moment.

Motion pictures have to move and so move us.

EDITING

If you want to understand film editing, you have to decide to resist what is most natural. You have to fight against the optical effects that compel us to see a film as a continuous whole and force yourself to count the cuts, to mark the constructed visual transitions that mask how the flow of one image is broken and interrupted by another. Most people have to train themselves to do this, but once you have done it, you develop the ability to see or not see the cuts of a film at will. The experience of "reading" a film closely like this is a bit like the experience of staring at a hologram or one of those plastic toys made for children that appear to be one thing, an Indian head, say, but then evolve into another when looked upon from a different angle, say a buffalo. We are trained, fooled if you will, by the powerful illusionary qualities of the cinema to see a narrative film as a seamless whole, while it is, in fact, pieced together from thousands of visual (and sound) fragments. To break free from the pull of the illusion to the point where you can see the constructedness of a film is absolutely necessary if you are to understand how a film creates meaning.

How many people have seen Alfred Hitchcock's *Psycho* and been absolutely horrified by the shower sequence in which Janet Leigh is slaughtered by a knife-wielding Anthony Perkins? The scene is so well known that a good many people have seen it or a parody of it who haven't even seen the entire film.

The curious terror that Hitchcock creates in that moment is largely a function of his mastery of editing techniques. The shower scene took seven days to shoot, as there were about seventy cameras used to film forty-five seconds of action. Each shot was carefully chosen from the hundreds of feet of footage shot and then spliced together with other shots in a long montage. In reality the knife never touched Janet Leigh nor the model used as her stand-in for some compositions; yet the impression created from the sequence when played out in the final version of the film is that we have just watched a vicious knife attack. That was certainly my first impression, seeing the film as a teenager. I couldn't believe that I had just seen so much graphic violence and nudity on network television, which is where I first saw the film. Later I would have opportunity to study the sequence closely and discover that what I thought I had seen was a mere illusion. Hitchcock never showed the knife actually cutting Janet Leigh, and she is never seen fully nude. It shouldn't surprise anyone that Hitchcock is considered one of cinema's great editing directors.

In the 1920s a Soviet filmmaker named Lev Kuleshov conducted a series of experiments designed to find out what the general laws of the then new art of film were that enabled moviemakers to create meaning. In his most famous experiment he juxtaposed an image of an expressionless actor with three evocative images—a bowl of soup, a dead woman in a coffin, and a girl with her teddy bear. He created three short film sequences cutting between the actor's face and each of the three images and then showed the shorts to different audiences. The audiences raved about the acting of the man, whom they thought had brilliantly responded to each image, showing hunger, or sorrow, or mirth.

Kuleshov's conclusion from this experiment was that the individual shot in a film has two distinct meanings—first, what it suggests in and of itself; and second, what it acquires from its pairing with other images. His experiments heavily influenced another Soviet filmmaker, Sergei Eisenstein, who became a leading propagandist for the new Soviet regime. His long Odessa Steps montage in the 1925 masterpiece *Battleship Potemkin* is one of the most famous and most affecting sequences in the history of film, as he conveys through montage the horror of a Czarist slaughter of citizens who gather to cheer the successful mutiny of the crew of the *Potemkin*.

The large point here is that much of film's power to move us and create meaning grows out of its editing, the manner in which images are spliced together. It is through editing that the filmmaker often tells us how to understand what we are being shown. Consider a couple more examples.

In 1981 Hugh Hudson created a wave of enthusiasm in the evangelical community with the success of his *Chariots of Fire*. The story, as mentioned above, is of two runners in the 1924 Olympics, one a Jewish student at Cambridge, Harold Abrahams, and the other a Scottish Presbyterian missionary to China, Eric Liddell. The stories of the two runners with their different backgrounds and motivations are told side by side, edited together if you will, until the stories merge in the final sequence at the Olympic Games.

In this final sequence, when Ian Charleson, as Liddell, wins the gold medal in the 400 meters, a race he was not originally scheduled to run, Hudson cuts from the images of Liddell running to reaction shots of the crowd cheering. Liddell is cheered by his sister and brother, a juxtaposition that suggests the pride he has created among those who love him most and a completion of one thread in the story. Then he is cheered in another crosscut by the Prince of Wales and members of the British Olympic committee who had tried to force him to run a 100-meter heat scheduled on a Sunday, a violation of the sabbath in Liddell's mind, the juxtaposition suggesting that God has honored Liddell for his integrity. Then finally a crosscut reveals an open-mouthed, shocked Harold Abrahams, the Jewish runner played by Ben Cross, who has won the 100-meter event that Liddell refused to run. That particular image, just one image, convinced many in the evangelical community that *Chariots of Fire* was a Christian movie showing the superiority of Liddell's faith to the proud Judaism of Abrahams. One image. In truth the image is somewhat more ambiguous than we evangelicals played it since Harold Abrahams's story is told in the film with much more energy than Liddell's. Hudson is celebrating both men, not particularly Liddell over Abrahams, and the powerful spirit of nationalism that they both embodied; yet by that one image, placed just so, he allowed a very distinct interpretation for the film in the minds of many evangelical viewers. The power of editing.

A more disturbing example of how editing can create our response to a film can be found in the 1998 film *Pleasantville*, directed by Gary Ross. Like several films that might be termed *postmodern*, this political allegory about two teenagers who enter the sappy world of a 1950s television show forces the viewer to notice the artifice of the film world by celebrating its own editing and effects. The world of Pleasantville, the town in the show, is completely black-and-white until the enlightened teenagers from "modern day" introduce creativity and true emotion (read: sex and self-indulgence), at which time the characters and objects of Pleasantville take on color. At one point a character wipes the black-and-white makeup off another who is trying to hide her color lest she face discrimination by the town's growing black-and-white racists.

This pretentious bit of Hollywood propaganda basically suggests that moral conservatives who bemoan the growing licentiousness in American culture are like the black-and-white robots of Pleasantville whose idea of a good time is eating stacks of pancakes and sucking down strawberry sodas. The teenagers who introduce the forbidden apple of liberated sex and rebellion from traditional authority are those who want life in the raw, as it is, unrestrained, from the heart, etc.

The film is disturbing on two levels. First, it is so cleverly composed and edited that most of the original viewers were taken by its skillful mechanics and thus accepted it as a whole without thinking through its rather subversive message. Then second, to reinforce the point being made, the "conservatives" of Pleasantville are equated with both the Ku Klux Klan and Nazis in several sequences in which the black-and-white mob threaten the poor, defenseless "colored" people who have been set free by modern values. These equations are made both through the compositions of several scenes that obviously mimic well-known footage of both the Klan and the Nazis and in the way these images are juxtaposed with those of the victimized "coloreds" led by the heroic teenagers.

In an era when most Americans get their information in

twenty-second television images and sound bites, the power of visual editing to create interpretations and attitudes should not be underestimated. By juxtaposing powerful images, a film-maker can say "this means that" without having to defend the assertion logically or historically. Both commercials on television and MTV follow this same principle.

But this is an entirely new discussion.

SOUND

If you want to do a simple exercise illustrating the importance of sound in films, take the 1980 Stanley Kubrick film *The Shining* and watch the opening sequence of a car driving down a winding road toward a remote hotel with your TV sound off and with a Strauss waltz playing from a record or CD. Then watch the same sequence with the film's actual sound. There will be little more to say to prove the importance of an appropriate sound track for a film.

Great directors are particular about the sound track attached to their films. Alfred Hitchcock's films continue to have force in part because of his collaboration with the brilliant composer Bernard Herrmann. Most great films have memorable scores. Think, for example, of *On the Waterfront* with its fine Leonard Bernstein score or *To Kill a Mockingbird* with Elmer Bernstein's moving score or *The Godfather* with its haunting Nino Rota score. It is often from hearing the music associated with a film that our memories of the film are later triggered.

There can be no overestimating the power of a film's sound track; yet that is only a part of the science of film sound. As with the visual images of a film, film sound is a construction. In very few films do you hear coming from the screen the precise sounds that occurred when the footage was shot. Even the voices we hear are often greatly altered. Actors are frequently called back to sound studios to respeak their lines after filming is complete so that these "better" sounding lines can be post-dubbed over existing visuals. Likewise the ambient or environmental sounds of a scene are usually either created synthetically or enhanced in some way. Adjustments are regularly made to the timbre of vocal sounds to make the wicked witch seem all the more wicked or to make our heroine seem all the more innocent or alluring.

Sounds can have thematic import in a film. In *Brief Encounter*, the great David Lean classic mentioned earlier, the sound of a train whistle and the roar of a passing commuter train suggest the emotional state of the main character, a housewife tempted to have an affair with a kindly doctor. As the film begins, the train whistle and roar initially only suggest place. By the film's end those same sounds have taken on new layers of meaning. In *A River Runs Through It*, the distorted voices of prisoners locked in a jail and overamplified sounds of the footsteps of a man going downstairs in that jail to recover his brother suggest the spiritual debasement of the imprisoned brother. In *Psycho* the shrill violins accompanying Norman Bates's attack in the shower scene replace the screams of the attacked woman and disturb us even more than the actual screams might.

Sound has always been prominent in film. Even silent films were to be accompanied by music. The music created moods but also often stood in for dialogue or ambient sound. In *City Lights* Charlie Chaplin used a muffled horn to replicate political speech to comic effect. Likewise, heroes and villains have always been given their own musical themes.

As with the filmic elements discussed above, the sound in a film has to be analyzed carefully to understand what a filmmaker is saying. This does not mean merely paying attention to dialogue, but considering all aspects of the film sound in their contexts.

ACTING

Perhaps the most pertinent comment that can be made about film acting is that it is always best not to notice it. If you notice the acting in a film, usually you do so because it is poor or is too stylized. Film is a medium that tends toward greater lifelikeness than other arts. If you are thinking in the middle of a film that you are watching a film, then in some way the experience is lessened. Watch an older film with a great stage actor playing a part and you usually detect something out of place in the performance. Laurence Olivier was one of the greatest stage actors of the twentieth century; yet when his films are seen by younger generations today, they usually come across as being either stuffy or overwrought. Olivier's rendition of Heathcliff from *Wuthering Heights* suffers in moments when he intentionally uses props, like a bedstead, as an actor might on stage where viewers sit at a great distance and need larger gestures. Likewise Olivier's Hamlet is a bit too articulate for modern viewers who would prefer Mel Gibson's spontaneity or the edginess of Kenneth Branagh. These "flaws" derive from the fact that Olivier is so obviously acting. Brilliantly acting perhaps; noticeably acting certainly.

Barbara Bel Geddes told the story of how Alfred Hitchcock demanded that she not act while performing in *Vertigo*. Bel Geddes was a highly acclaimed stage actress at the time, but Hitchcock went so far as to tell her how to move her head and eyes in specific scenes. The method would never work on stage, but it resulted in a great film performance.

To understand film acting, several things must be understood. First, it is important not to confuse a great performance by a director with a great performance by an actress or actor. Barbara Bel Geddes was a great actress, but her success in *Vertigo* was a result of a great performance by Hitchcock. On the other hand, Michael Curtiz was merely a competent director whose stock increased when Humphrey Bogart turned in one of the most interesting performances ever filmed in *Casablanca*. Recall the Kuleshov Effect here. If a film is edited well, it may seem that a performer is performing when he is merely standing still and gazing off in the distance. Sometimes what seems like creative invention by a performer is nothing more than obeying orders well. A great performance is much more.

A good example of genuine creative invention on a performance level would be any Charlie Chaplin feature. Chaplin directed his own films but did very little in the way of cinematography or editing that would be termed great. What he did was create a persona before the camera that touched millions of people and that has never been replicated. Chaplin would shoot reels and reels of footage when preparing his films to allow himself to explore fully all the performance possibilities in a particular scene. Often he would start a scene with nothing more than a prop and one sight gag, and from this create a long comic sequence.

The second issue to consider when regarding film acting is style. There are basically two distinct approaches that can be taken to an individual role. One is script-driven; the other is character-driven. An actor can be a brilliant interpreter of lines and movements that exist on a page. Or an actor can create the page during the performance. Some performers who fall into the latter group would be Marlon Brando, James Dean, and Robert DeNiro. Their films typically have a very immediate quality to them, and their performances seem spontaneous. Other actors are brilliant interpreters of scripts—for example, Anthony Hopkins, Gwyneth Paltrow, or Meryl Streep. Like all stylistic matters, an individual performance must be evaluated with consideration of what exactly the actor is trying to do. Also, the question of appropriateness must be raised—how appropriate is the style of performance to the individual film vehicle?

The third issue is the physical performance. Often what is missed in great acting is how much of the whole body is involved. Watch Meryl Streep or Anthony Hopkins when they are not speaking and you will see the performance continue. With lesser performers, one often feels they are waiting for their next lines. Ever wonder why an actress or actor whose career seems so promising from one film disappears into obscurity or slides into television roles? Often the answer is in their inability to follow through on a performance in more challenging roles. Their ability is limited to their words and their face. Many Green Bay fans were horrified at Brett Favre's performance as an actor in *There's Something About Mary* because the graceful, innovative quarterback looked stiff as a goalpost on screen. What often looks fluid and natural in film is the product of a great and practiced talent exerting her- or himself to the maximum. It is said that Tom Cruise developed an ulcer as a result of his repeated efforts to walk as Stanley Kubrick requested in *Eyes Wide Shut*.

The final issue is that of the star phenomenon. Often what is perceived as great acting in film is little more than the actor's own dramatic charisma. This is a bit hard to define, but we are all familiar with the reality. Some performers in film develop a cult following because they grow out of their individual roles into some larger icon that has resonance with popular culture. The obvious example here would be Marilyn Monroe. Who could say that her appeal had to do only with her acting skills or her beauty? She appealed as an icon. She stood for something beyond her roles and films. Jimmy Stewart had such an appeal, as did John Wayne. Today we might attribute this kind of iconic appeal to Harrison Ford or Meg Ryan or Sylvester Stallone.

They have each struck a chord with pop culture; yet this does not necessarily mean they are performing brilliantly. You might love a particular film today because you feel an affinity with a favorite star performing in it, not because it is a particularly good film with good performances. Evaluating a film can be a complex business, and there is always a temptation to pretend that we can all do it equally well.

STORY

Although a film can be effective without a great story (recall the earlier discussion regarding written literature versus film art), most truly great films do have compelling stories. Scan a list of the AFI's 100 top films and you will be hard-pressed to find one that doesn't revolve around some significant human theme like courage or patriotism or redemption or betrayal or maturation or family love. There is much more to these films than a good story, but plot and theme are packaged in interesting, original ways.

What would be the legacy of *Citizen Kane* if not for the revelation about Rosebud? Who could imagine *E.T.* being anywhere near as powerful as it is without the poignant ending with the boy and the creature? Who hasn't been intrigued by the perverse possibility of the world actually producing a "Manchurian Candidate"?

Great stories tell us about our own lives, and they will tell our children about their lives. They are universal in appeal. They teach and uplift, even when tragic. A film like *Silence of the Lambs* or *Easy Rider* may have a certain generational appeal and show up for a time on lists like the one generated by the AFI, but because the stories are ultimately ugly and pointless or downright absurd, they will lose their appeal through time.

When evaluating a good story in a film, one considers the

originality of the concept, the quality of the writing, and the manipulation of audience expectations. But overall we look for something that immerses us in the details of the human condition and brings us to see something valuable: Truth. And we look for respect—a respect of who we are as individuals living by the mercy of God in a fallen world, longing for a redemption that only God can provide. This is so important a concept, it deserves its own chapter.

CHAPTER THREE

"WHATEVER IS TRUE"

ⓢ

Finally, brethren, whatever is true, whatever is honorable, whatever is right, whatever is pure, whatever is lovely, whatever is of good repute, if there is any excellence and if anything worthy of praise, dwell on these things.
—*Philippians 4:8,* NASB

A few years back a fine independent film came out called *The Big Night* (1996) about two brothers trying to make a go of an Italian restaurant in a city neighborhood. The older brother, Primo, is a chef who will not compromise his cooking for the sake of making money. The younger brother, Secondo, is the restaurant manager who must face the hard business realities of trying to pay the mortgage and compete with a sportier restaurant on the same block. The conflict proposed in the film is whether it is better to fail with dignity or to succeed through personal compromise. The film handles the subject humorously, yet truthfully and poignantly. Although *The Big Night* was not heavily promoted by the industry, it received good reviews from film experts and had a small market following.

A couple years later a similar little film came out and

received good reviews, this one an Irish production called *Waking Ned Divine*, the story of a man from a small community in Ireland who wins a substantial lottery but dies from shock in his chair when his winning number is read on television. Two friends find him and decide to hide the fact of his death, one of them taking his place in a scam to secure the lottery winnings for the town. The men fool the authorities and collect and distribute the money equally to the fifty-some local residents, who celebrate and, we are led to assume, live happily ever after with their newfound prosperity. Along the way, a spoil-sport woman who tries to break up the party by exposing the men is comically thwarted.

Now, speaking hypothetically, if all artistic matters in the two films are the same—equal technical merit, originality, fulfillment of intent, etc.—which would be the better film? Many people would have to conclude that *The Big Night* would be the better film, all else being equal, because its story is more significant and morally sound. *The Big Night* teaches something valuable about art and life—integrity. *Waking Ned Divine* entertains us with the playing out of a common wish, but leaves behind nothing of great use beyond a smile.

If you agree with this conclusion, you are doing so on the basis of two assumptions about life and art. You are suggesting that a goal of life is to become a better person, and you are suggesting that a goal of art is, likewise, to make us better people.

Here is where a Christian may be forced to part company with many of those who do not share in the faith, because our Christian faith compels us to make just these assumptions. The chief end of man, as the old creed tells us, "is to glorify God," and what better way to bring glory to God than to make of our lives something beautiful? Likewise, the apostle Paul tells us that whatever we "do" (1 Corinthians 10:31) is also to be for God's glory, and thus how can an artist not intend on some level to bless people with what he does, his art?

I don't want to take this to the extreme of a Leo Tolstoy, for example, who suggested that all art is to promote the universal brotherhood of man, a position that led him to misunderstand the greatest Christian writer of his own age, Fyodor Dostoyevsky. But I do mean to suggest that as Christians it is appropriate to value some art more highly than other art on the basis of its subject matter. Certainly, as argued in an earlier chapter, art doesn't have to be overtly religious or moral in tone to have merit. But great art does tend to have at its core great subjects; and about those great subjects, great artists have much of worth to say.

It should likewise be noted here that Christians are not alone in evaluating certain films on the basis of content. Most people do this in any case, whether Christian or not. The feminist viewer values films like *The Piano* or *Thelma and Louise* because these films attack patriarchal culture and promote women's issues. Marxists are enamored with films about the evils of capitalism like *Metropolis* or *Blue Collar*. Homosexuals praise Billy Wilder's *Some Like It Hot* or the more recent *Philadelphia*. Academics these days always must state their politics before engaging in textual analysis; so as Christians we needn't blush at the immodesty of stating up front what we consider good. We should, in fact, do so gladly; after all, it is part of our witness to the world.

Yet, if Christians do stand up and advocate some standard of decency regarding the content of film, we can be assured of being accused of promoting censorship. And perhaps for good reason. Christians have tended to respond to controversial films by either actively protesting them with placards and angry letters or via some organized boycott. The outrage over Martin

Scorsese's *The Last Temptation of Christ* would be a good case in point.

The problem seems to be that where content is concerned, Christians tend to respond by rule and not by principle. And operating primarily by rule, we find ourselves evaluating the content of a film on a moralistic scale based on the depiction of violence and sexuality. After all, these transgressions are in some sense quantifiable. It is possible to count the deaths that occur in a film, and we can certainly notice when an actor or actress gets undressed.

However, as understandable as it is that good people are upset about the excesses of modern film, it is very difficult to make binding rules about what any art should or should not do. Mark Twain's novel *Huckleberry Finn* contains over 200 usages of the word *nigger*. Since this word is highly offensive, numerous American school districts and libraries have removed the book from circulation. The decisions have been made by the rule that literature with offensive terms should not be given to children. Yet *Huckleberry Finn* is a novel that actually promotes racial understanding. The best character in the book is Huck's friend, the slave Jim; and the climax of the story occurs when Huck realizes he cannot abide by the law and return Jim to slavery.

Even though violence and sexuality in film can produce exceedingly bad results due to the voyeuristic aspects of the cinema experience, it is still impossible to make consistent rules about what an individual film ought not or ought to do. There is, after all, a place for violence and sexuality in art, if art is to be truthful. All you have to do to recognize this is read the Old Testament. Certain acts of human violence are celebrated in Scripture: Think of Deborah's song in which she celebrates Jael's pinning Sisera to the ground with a tent peg through the forehead—"Most blessed of women be Jael. . . . She struck Sisera, she crushed his head, she shattered and pierced his temple" (Judges 5:24, 26, NIV). Likewise, only the most prudish reader will read the Song of Solomon without acknowledging the overtly sexual nature of some of the descriptive passages and metaphors—"Let me see your form, let me hear your voice; for your voice is sweet, and your form is lovely" (Song of Songs 2:14, NASB).

Some of the greatest literary masterpieces and the most Christian have difficult moments. Dante's hell is an awfully rough place. Milton has Adam and Eve drink their fill of carnal pleasures after their sin in *Paradise Lost*. Dostoyevsky's Raskolnikov viciously ax-murders a pawnbroker and her sister before finally repenting in *Crime and Punishment*. Hugo makes plain how Cosette's mother Fantine finances her daughter's upbringing in *Les Miserables*. Dickens graphically describes how Bill Sikes bludgeons to death his prostitute-mistress Nancy in *Oliver Twist*. Flannery O'Connor seemed unable to bring a short story to a conclusion without an act of violence committed. Likewise, some of the best and most Christian films ever made have their rough moments—*Andrei Rublev, Black Robe, The Gospel According to St. Matthew*, to name three.

The problem is not so much the presence of violence and sexuality in film; the problem is how and why the violence and sexuality are played out as they are. Unfortunately, here is where Christians need to think in terms of principles and not rules. Each film needs to be viewed according to its own special design.

Again, there is no question that our American film industry has lost sight of any reasonable standard of decency and that any God-fearing man or woman should be appalled at the content of many films. (We are not alone in this problem either, for the

French film industry has likewise sunk to new lows.) God has seemingly withdrawn His hand and allowed us to slide into greater and greater depravity, and the temptation is indeed great to shake the dust off our feet and walk away from the entire entertainment industry. Yet, if we want to be salt and light for the people who create, promote, and watch film, or for that matter for our own children who live in a "movie-made culture," we need at the very least to address the problem precisely, using our God-given reason and our Bibles.

Any number of films—for example, "teen slasher" films like *Scream* or *I Know What You Did Last Summer* or *Urban Legend* or a fantasy-action film like *Blade*—should certainly be labeled pornographic and decried for the way violence and sex are used for effect, pornographic in the wider sense of presenting explicit visual images purely to arouse. More often than not, however, otherwise reasonable films contain isolated moments of pornography designed to draw into the theater a certain crowd—adolescents and young adults. Just about every light romance does this. I'm not sure we should respond to both types of film in the same way. We ought to make discriminations between films that have no redeeming value and those that simply lack consistent taste.

Likewise we need to discriminate between a director like Paul Verhoeven (*Basic Instinct* and *Striptease*) who revels in the seedy and decadent, the way a brothel madam might, and a director like Martin Scorsese (*Taxi Driver* and *Casino*) who, whether misguidedly or not, is trying to portray truthfully an ugly element in American society for the sake of a larger message. One of the best films of the nineties is Stephen Spielberg's *Schindler's List*, a film that all Christians should commend for its powerful moral statements, and yet a film that is at times very difficult to watch.

Beyond this, we need to recognize that there are more corrosive messages in film than the violent and sexual ones. After all, some people live through wars and others who are poor live and sleep in close quarters. Worse things can happen to a young man than seeing a woman's breasts in a film, which is not to say that he should, of course. He is perhaps in even more danger because of the messages of universal tolerance or because of the materialism that so many films both explicitly and implicitly promote. When Jesus warned us that we cannot serve God and mammon, He was addressing sins more in the range of covetousness, jealousy, envy, and pride than He was sins in the range of murder and adultery. I have always been amazed at the selective Puritanism of so many Christians who find everything wrong with sins of the flesh but little wrong with sins like greed or gossip.

What Paul advocates in that well-known passage in Philippians 4:8, as applied to this topic, is not that we condemn violence and sexuality in art wherever it be found, but rather that we promote and dwell on art's positives—the good, true, noble, and praiseworthy. A film criticism that deals only in negative rules is hardly "Christian," unless we define Christianity by some Victorian moral standard. Paul tells us to fill our minds with particular things—"whatever is true, whatever is honorable, whatever is right, whatever is pure, whatever is lovely, whatever is of good repute, if there is any excellence, and if anything worthy of praise." We need to avoid the tunnel vision that translates the Christian life into a set of "do not" laws and learn instead to live by redeeming every experience through the truth of Jesus Christ. Paul saw many horrible things while in prison and during his travels, but his eyes always focused ahead of his troubles on the "goal for the prize of the upward call of God in Jesus Christ" (Philippians 3:14, NASB). Christians need to concentrate on the good in many films. And as for the bad, it might serve as a reminder that the dreams Hollywood tries to convince us are true can *never* come true in a fallen world that so desperately needs to embrace the love of Jesus Christ.

Now all of this is not to suggest that we should somehow drop our guard and watch every movie that comes out, asking Jesus to help us learn truth through them. The Scripture is full of commands that the people of God pursue moral purity by avoiding or cutting off or fleeing from bad influences. James says that pure and undefiled religion means "to keep oneself unstained by the world" (James 1:27, NASB). Certainly this involves selecting our pleasures carefully. After all, who will guard your soul? Certainly not the entertainment industry itself, which seeks often to profit by playing on your weaknesses, and certainly not artists, whose main concern is personal expression.

One of the most recognized sections of John Bunyan's great classic *Pilgrim's Progress* finds Christian and his friend Faithful in the town of Vanity Fair. In this town all the world's goods are on display for sale—"houses, lands, trades, places, honours, preferments, titles, countries, kingdoms, lusts, pleasures, and delights of all sorts. . . ." Bunyan's point is to show how the world seeks to pull us off the road to heaven by selling us "happiness" in some package. He takes the idea from Solomon's conclusions to his search for meaning in the book of Ecclesiastes. Solomon says that all is vanity when sought as an end in itself, and therefore "the whole duty of man" (12:13, NIV) is to fear God and keep His commandments. Bunyan saw the pursuit of vanities in his day as a kind of carnival of waste and folly, and what is particularly noteworthy in Bunyan's honest vision of Vanity Fair is that he adds to the list of sale items the common entertainments of his day—"jugglings . . . games, plays, fools, apes. . . ." One can only imagine what he would add were he living now and not in the seventeenth century. Certainly film would be mentioned. He might even have Christian tempted at a movie house in a separate chapter.

We ought to take care how we watch movies and what those movies tell us.

Now, I have to admit that my job makes it impossible for me to be as selective as I often recommend that others be. I see a wide range of films so that when students ask my opinions I can offer a thoughtful answer. Yet, I always make clear that people should take care when spending time with strangers in dark rooms. In general it is certainly far better for the soul to watch a film that says something worthwhile than it is to have to wade through sewage in search of the drain stopper. And it is certainly always incumbent upon us to think through the films we see, rather than merely reacting to them emotionally.

Of course, to be thoughtful about "entertainment" might get you labeled overly serious in this day and age, even by other Christians. But remember, "What shall it profit a man, if he gain the whole world, and lose his own soul?" (Mark 8:36, KJV). It sounds cranky, but it is certainly true that a man can lose his soul in a movie house. A woman can too.

The challenge, then, is to learn what is "good" content in a film and how to find it.

I wouldn't recommend listening to industry experts, most of whom are either too tied to the money or the politics of the industry to be objective. Simply consider how the American Film Institute listed in its top 100 films fifteen that most good parents would hesitate to let their children see—*Annie Hall, Bonnie and Clyde, A Clockwork Orange, Easy Rider, Fargo, The Godfather, Goodfellas, The Graduate, Midnight Cowboy, Network, Platoon, Pulp Fiction, Raging Bull, The Silence of the Lambs,* and *Taxi Driver.* Of the novels that one might consider classics, very few have content too strong for children, but somehow we are led by the prestigious AFI to believe that 15% of the truly great films are unfit for children.

The list is biased, of course. There are fifty films that could have been chosen instead of the fifteen listed above, especially from the studio era (circa 1930-1960) when the federally enforced Production Code kept Hollywood's toe on the moral line, films like *Cheyenne Autumn* or *Top Hat* or *Angels with Dirty Faces* or *A Tree Grows in Brooklyn* or *The Shop Around the Corner* or *The Mortal Storm*. Going back even further to the silent era, the AFI could have chosen *Sunrise* or *The General* or *Broken Blossoms* or *Safety Last* or several other remarkable films. Or taking another approach, instead of *Taxi Driver* and *Raging Bull*, the Martin Scorsese film *Age of Innocence* might have been chosen. It lacks the extremely rough contents of the other two films while exceeding them in many regards stylistically and technically.

Looking at the AFI list from the perspective of content underlines the moral degeneration we have undergone culturally. There was a time, after all, when negative content in art was seen as a negative thing for society. Scholars now seem to think that any kind of principle imposed upon artists to hold them accountable to standards of common decency is too difficult to define. It is only a recent contribution to the development of western civilization to think that because a social task is difficult we shouldn't attempt it.

The great fallacy promoted by film scholars and the film industry is the notion that films merely reflect the culture and therefore cannot be considered a corrosive to society. People who say such things fail to understand that while artists in the western tradition have always striven to tell the truth, they have also typically created worlds somewhat better than our own.

Heroes and villains have tended to be larger than life in art. Maidens were rather more beautiful and clever, providence a shade more precise. At least this had been the tendency prior to the late twentieth century, when it became fashionable to create art that is a little *less* than real life. This seems to be what is happening in contemporary film. Characters have less grace and less conscience; their acts are more cruel and their language more crude. When you see even some very fine films from the last few decades, like the *Godfather* films, you cannot help but feel the downward pull of the story. This is a world made a little worse than the one we know.

The contrast is sharp between many of the "modern classics" in films like *The Godfather* or *Taxi Driver* or *Fargo* and films from, say, the mid-thirties and forties. Take, for example, one of the best films from that period, Frank Capra's *Mr. Smith Goes to Washington* (1939), an appropriate choice on the AFI list. Frank Capra is the same director who made the Christmas classic *It's a Wonderful Life* (1946). At his peak in the thirties and forties, Capra made a string of memorable films beyond these two, including *Lady for a Day, It Happened One Night, Mr. Deeds Goes to Town, You Can't Take It with You,* and *Arsenic and Old Lace.* Virtually all of Capra's films deal in some measure with the clash between idealism and bitter experience. Many have the quality of a parable, posing a moral problem and answering it with a story—think of George Bailey in *It's a Wonderful Life* wondering if he should ever have been born and then finding out what his town would have been like without his efforts.

Mr. Smith Goes to Washington is an illustration of the kind of great film you find during the studio era that would probably never get made now because it is too nice. I am reminded of an experience I had in graduate school the year that *Chariots of*

Fire came out and won the Academy Award. One of my advisors disliked the film intensely, and when I asked why, she said it was because the film was "so nationalistic." The implication was that had the film attacked Britain instead of celebrating her people and spirit, it would have been a better work of art. The reverse is true, of course. The patriotism of Leni Riefenstahl's propagandistic *Triumph of the Will* (Germany, 1935) is certainly a bad thing in that it paints the Third Reich as a benevolent people's movement. Patriotism is a good thing, however, when directed at worthy subjects and historical events. *Mr. Smith Goes to Washington* is a great film in large part because it stirs patriotism directed correctly (that is, unless you regret America's democratic heritage).

It is the story of a young and idealistic young leader who comes to Washington as a Senate appointee and finds a web of corruption centered in his own state. Rather than giving up because of the large odds against positive change, he filibusters the Senate to prevent a corrupt bill from going forward and wins the day—and the girl, a newspaper reporter who follows his story and falls in love with him.

The most memorable scene in the film occurs at the point when the Senator, Jefferson Smith, has been framed by the political machine he opposes and is near the point of defeat, ready to return to his state and give up any hope for a better America. With suitcases in hand he goes to the Lincoln Memorial and sits in the shadow of the monument of the great president. There Clarissa, the girl, finds him in this state of utter discouragement and reminds him of all the boys back home counting on him ("When you get back home, what will you tell those kids?") and of the great tradition of American heroes (Washington, Jefferson, Lincoln) who fought against insurmountable odds to establish our nation and of the great heritage of small-town

America that he, Jefferson Smith, represents. And, in so many words, she lets him know of her love. The encouragement revives his courage and enables him to return to the Senate floor to fight for his beliefs by staging a one-man filibuster.

Visually, it is a stunning scene, played out in high contrast lighting emphasizing the conflict in Jefferson Smith's (James Stewart's) face and the beauty of Clarisse (Jean Arthur) and all she represents. The elements are simple—the towering presence of Lincoln seated at the monument, the small man struggling to emulate him, the woman pushing him on; yet each element stands for so much more than the silhouetted images that we see. In terms of "pure cinema," film as a primarily visual medium, you would be hard-pressed to find a better cinematographic sequence than this one from *Mr. Smith*. But the sequence gains its tremendous force through the ideas conveyed by those images.

Jean Arthur encourages James Stewart to fight for the good in Frank Capra's *Mr. Smith Goes to Washington* (1939).

Mr. Smith Goes to Washington makes us want to preserve the good of our past and reinvent that good in our present. It celebrates the small man of integrity, love based on respect, community, courage, hope, and conscience. It is beautifully made certainly—with crisp and memorable dialogue, vivid characterizations, striking compositions. But it is also about something beautiful—a political ideal that created in America a nation so appealing that immigrants came here at significant risk to create a better life for themselves and their children.

And this is the point. Great films promote great things and tell great stories. They have a fundamental integrity, a truthfulness in the way they portray the deeds and the dreams of men and women created by our loving God. They help us to be wiser and more compassionate. They encourage us toward the good.

Furthermore, Capra's film, although not overtly Christian, bases its premise on the plight of a righteous man in a corrupted world, a central issue in Scripture. It suggests that the individual good man must find courage from the great men who lived before. It shows how good triumphs through perseverance and suffering. It describes love based on character. And in these and many other ways it illustrates much that we uphold as Christian people. Like so much of this country's early art, while not addressing religious issues directly, it exhales the Christianity that established our nation.

Despite the loud voices of our culture, content does matter in art, and particularly in the powerful art of film. And there are absolutes that define what good content is, those that have been traditionally labeled by Christian western civilization as "virtues"—honor, kindness, brotherly love, faithfulness, perseverance, valor, pity, repentance . . . A sunrise simply is a beautiful thing. A mother's hug comforts us. Most children want a dog. *God has created a world with absolutes.* When Paul tells us to hold on to the good, he assumes we all know what the good is. A film about a psychotic taxi driver obsessed with saving a teen prostitute, even if made by a talent like Michelangelo's, is still going to be distasteful in the main (Martin Scorsese's *Taxi Driver*). Not a good. Preferable would be a film by a lesser talent about a lonely butcher who meets a plain but gentle woman and decides to marry her, despite the mockery of his friends. Ever hear of the Academy Award winner from 1955, *Marty*?

CHAPTER FOUR

WHAT'S LOVE GOT TO DO WITH IT?

֍

Leo Tolstoy wrote the great novel *Anna Karenina* after reading a newspaper account of a society woman who had committed suicide. Tolstoy asked himself why a woman of her class and education and seeming comfort would fall to so desperate an act. In chasing this question *why*, Tolstoy created a novel that perhaps teaches more about the motivations of the human heart than any other work of fiction has or ever will.

The question *why* can not only lead to great literature, it can also enhance the study of literature. Students, for example, often know many facts about certain authors. They might know, for instance, that John Milton wrote *Paradise Lost* in the seventeenth century and that the epic is about the Fall and that Milton was blind when he wrote it, but the simple question *why* will often elude them. *Why* is it important to know this? *Why* is *Paradise Lost* considered so great? Having a mind full of discrete facts might get you through a test, but it doesn't guarantee genuine understanding.

The question *why* proves especially useful in the study of film.

Since film is a mass-produced commodity as well as an art form, the largest number of films produced each year are highly formulaic and predictable. The investors who back the production companies that create popular films, such as Paramount or United Artists, prefer to have their investments guaranteed. Given the choice between a tried and true formula film with proven stars in the key roles and an innovative film with new faces, most financiers, Wall Street types, would certainly choose the sure bet, the formula film. This phenomenon is the Hollywood story. Actors and directors push for originality, while the money behind the film pushes for guarantees. And who can blame either side? We expect artists to have integrity in their work, and we expect bankers, who advance several million dollars to make a film, to be prudent.

The many formula films made each year—horror films, adventure thrillers, science-fiction fantasies, war dramas, love stories, etc.—are called *genre* films. They are *generic* products that have proven to sell. Mad slasher terrorizes group of promiscuous adolescents, killing them all in brutal fashion, until he meets the one pure girl who thwarts him. Power mad foreign terrorist takes over important building (or plane or ship) and threatens wholesale murder, but one lone hero fights and defeats him. Spacecraft enters bizarre warp in space and discovers a mode of evil ready to spread and infect the universe. Reluctant soldier shows uncommon valor despite pointless cruelty of war. Two seemingly unlikely individuals meet, fall in love, face innumerable barriers to their love, and then come together again for good.

There is a comical moment in the 1992 Robert Altman film *The Player* when a production executive in a film studio demonstrates how easily he can compose film plots from the front page headlines of a newspaper. Each headline—building burns, stocks fall, child lost—suggests a conflict that can be approached through some film formula or other. The scene is effective because true.

Genre films are easily conceived and have a guaranteed market, thus returning a predictable return on their original financial investment. *Halloween 8*, should it be made, will probably turn a profit, irregardless of how awful it may prove to be. The studio producing the film will set a budget appropriate for the market and then advertise through trailers and newspaper promos to get teens into the theaters. An idiosyncratic film like *Forrest Gump*, on the other hand, is much more risky because it represents a new commodity with an unpredictable appeal.

The system for promoting films is so well refined that even the poorest products will get some audience. We have all been victimized by this. Just last night my wife and I were lured by a good trailer to see one of the worst movies in quite some time, a repugnant mystery/thriller called *The General's Daughter*, a film with an outrageous plot that featured a young woman pleading for her father's understanding and love while staked naked to the ground, spread-eagled, by tent pegs. And Hollywood types wonder why family-oriented folk point an accusing finger!

If you look through the movie section of your local paper this Sunday, you will notice how formulaic most of the films playing at the theaters are. You could choose to see one based on a review and your liking of the genre, or you could throw the paper down in disgust. Whichever course you choose, you might momentarily pause and ask a key question: *Why* these same stories over and over again? *Why* not something new?

This is the question that should be particularly interesting for Christians in a subject area that might otherwise hold little interest. The concept of the genre is easy enough to understand, but the success of certain types of film over others is less so. *Why* do

American teens want to go to the theater to see a slasher film like *Scream*? The easy answer is that the culture is depraved and addicted to violence, but this answer is the same as our initial response to a case of shoplifting might be. It states the most obvious fact and passes quick and easy judgment. *Scream* is bad, our culture is bad, our kids are in jeopardy; let's think of how we can protect them.

All that might be true, but the conclusions are too easy and tend to lead us toward self-righteousness, not understanding.

Taking *Scream* for an example, the issue is not so much the fact of its violence; the issue is why *this* story pattern should have *this* appeal for American young people at *this* particular historical moment. If we can answer that, and some scholars have done a pretty decent job, we might better understand the minds of young people today, and we might be better able to explain to them the good news of the Gospel.

Scream (like most of the slasher films that have done so well at the box office since Hitchcock's *Psycho* broke the ground originally in 1960) appeals because of its assumptions about random evil in American society, the effects of the breakdown of the American family, and the dangers of unchecked *male* sexuality in youth culture. Like a nightmare the genre plays out certain anxieties, not those of individuals but those of a group, in a controllable context (the film itself, which I choose to watch and which has a fixed beginning and end). In fact, *Scream* plays out these social fears self-consciously. In the film a group of teens who are addicted to horror films and who know all the rules of the genre become both killers and victims in a game of fright that they choose to play. In the opening scene a beautiful young woman, home alone, gets a phone call from a man who tries to seduce and then terrify her. The girl, played by Drew Barrymore (who first entered film, significantly, as the

sweet and innocent daughter in *E.T.*), at first responds posi-
tively to the caller, thinking the call a friendly joke, part of the
game that she and her teen friends are playing. When she realizes that the call is not "a game," she becomes frightened and
tries to forestall the inevitable. The ensuing sequence in which
she is stalked and murdered is one of the most disturbing in the
entire horror genre.

Translated, in an age when young girls fear rape perhaps
more than ever before, having been left at home alone by the
failure of parents to hold together a family, slasher films play out
the fear in the worst case imaginable. Nothing can prevent the
inevitable bloodbath, not even knowing that it is on the way as
in *Scream*. The trademark films of the genre (*Halloween, Friday
the 13th, The Texas Chainsaw Massacre, Nightmare on Elm
Street*) feature a male stalker who wields a long knife (read in
Freud) and kills every teenager he finds who is sexually active.
The last intended victim, still a virgin, manages to escape after
a terrifying ordeal. In another strand of the genre, the formula
gets reversed, and a sexually wronged woman seeks vengeance
on the man or men guilty (*Play Misty for Me, Fatal Attraction,
The Hand That Rocks the Cradle*). Watching the film in the con-
trolled laboratory of the theater becomes a bit like an exor-
cism—you conjure the demon in order to destroy it (although
the film demons, at least the male ones, like Frankenstein, seem
always to escape the burning windmill).

I wouldn't recommend that anyone go to any of the films just
mentioned, but I think it is a mistake for Christians to dismiss
them without thought. These films teach us some very valuable
lessons about our world. In particular this horror/slasher genre
teaches us that many young people are simply afraid of the consequences of the sexual freedom they have been pushed to
accept. Irregardless of the motives of the producers of the indi-

vidual films, the popularity of them is socially telling. To a
Christian this popularity might suggest that sexual freedom has
left more broken than happy young people, and therefore more
young people who might respond to Jesus.

Other film genres provide other insights when the question
why is applied. *Why*, for instance, have film westerns lost their
popularity? Westerns are, after all, the most distinctively
American literary and film genre, traceable to the popularity of
James Fennimore Cooper's *Leatherstocking Tales* of the mid-
nineteenth century, a genre that plays out our historical and cultural identity more than any other. The first American narrative
film was *The Great Train Robbery*, a 1903 western, and the
genre quickly became the most-often filmed through the 1920s
and then again from the 1940s to the 1960s.

But where have they gone? Granted, a few dark westerns
have appeared over the past few decades like *Young Guns*,

John Wayne completes the search in John Ford's great western *The Searchers*
(1956). The iconography of the western is all present in this one image.

Lonesome Dove, Dances with Wolves, and *Tombstone.* But these few lack the texture and vitality of the old John Ford, Budd Boetticher, Howard Hawks films.

Two things seem to have happened. First, Americans have lost their somewhat mythic view of the settling of the West. Since the American family structure has largely disintegrated, the notion of the proud *home*stead pushing civilization through the wilderness has lost its force. Likewise, historical revisions have made us question the entire endeavor of settling an already settled land. (After all, weren't Indians the true Americans?) The popularity of Kevin Costner's *Dances with Wolves* testifies to this. In Costner's Academy Award-winning film, the western genre gets stood on its head in that the idealized homestead is that of the Native Americans while the hostile savages are the white Europeans.

Second, the western story pattern got transcribed onto the science-fiction genre with the *Star Trek* and *Star Wars* movies. Space is "the new frontier" in recent film. In an odd way since the western is such a great story, rather than lose it we have moved it from the realm of historical myth to the realm of fantasy. Few people really believe America will stretch her vision of "the land of the free" beyond Mars; yet creating the possibility imaginatively does make for great entertainment.

Why should Christians take note of this change in a film genre? For several reasons, not the least of which is that perhaps now we can finally learn that the future of Christianity is not bound up in the prosperity of this country. Also, we might remember what we read in Proverbs: "Where there is no vision, the people perish" (29:18, KJV). Having lost faith in the history and identity of this country as passed down for 200 years, Americans for the most part now seem to have lost faith in the possibility of a good, nurturing society. If this is indeed true, then churches in America face a challenge to live out Christian community as never before.

A similar conclusion might be drawn regarding the disappearance of musicals over the last two or three decades. The thirties (Astaire and Rogers, *42nd Street, The Wizard of Oz*) and the fifties and early sixties (Gene Kelly, *Singing in the Rain, An American in Paris, Gigi, West Side Story, The Sound of Music*) were the heydays of the great musical. Now young people chuckle when the music starts playing in these older films. Extended rock videos like Prince's *Purple Rain* or teen dance films like *Saturday Night Fever, Flashdance, Grease, Dirty Dancing,* and *Footloose* are as close as we have come to the great older films in recent years. Again, the heart and soul has gone out of the genre. Its celebration of idealized love and pure, American exuberance no longer seem to fit the cultural mood.

Why has this happened? The sixties, Kennedy's assassination, Vietnam, the growing drug culture, creeping materialism—perhaps all of these and more. *Why* should we Christians take note? Perhaps because Christianity offers the very thing that seems to be lacking in modern America—joy. Maybe the death of the musical is a signal that Christians need to show more joy in all circumstances like Paul did in that Roman prison in Philippi. It is so easy at times to fall into the pessimism of those among whom we live. Our worship services may have great energy, but perhaps the joy never leaks out when we leave. We might consider opening the back doors of the church during the service to bring the wonders of reconciliation to our stagnant streets. We worship for the most part in the safest of ways and then keep silent about it.

A genre that has not declined but has grown in popularity over the past two decades is the action/thriller featuring the one brave hero who single-handedly turns back a band of terrorists or revolutionaries bent on an act of mass destruction. Sylvester Stallone became the prototype of this hero in the *Rambo* films. Jean-Claude Van Damme, Steven Segal, Arnold Schwarzenegger, and Bruce Willis have built their careers on these roles, but other actors with greater range have taken them on as well—Harrison Ford in *Air Force One*, Nicolas Cage in *Con Air*, and Christian Slater in *Broken Arrow*, to name just three.

A film of this genre, say *Die Hard*, blends elements from the western and martial arts films and comic book remakes (think *Batman*) in a semi-parody of the old stories about the heroic rugged individualist who protects the town from marauders. The odds are stacked far too high against the hero for any viewer to consider the story plausible. At least in an old western like *High Noon* the odds of one Gary Cooper (with an assist from Grace Kelly) against four bad guys remains reasonable. Here, however, one unarmed hero will go up against two dozen fully armed and trained killers, and of course win in the end. The pleasure stems from the implausibility of the story—the more plates of glass the hero crashes through in the course of the action, the better the film.

As with the musical, these films signal a loss in our culture. We have lost hope for real solutions to problems like international terror and organized crime. The heroes of the old westerns were men of a type that we believed did exist. Shane might not have existed, but rugged gunslingers who cared about pioneer settlers being safe from greedy ranchers probably did. Natty Bumppo, the hero of James Fennimore Cooper's novels and prototype for Michael Mann's hero in the popular film *The Last of the Mohicans*, is a bit too good to be true. Yet, we believe (or believed) that there were independent men who lived with one foot in the frontier and one in the settlements, who made possible the success of the early colonists and who pushed the country's interests westward. We did, after all, have our John Smiths and our Daniel Boones and our Wild Bills. They might have been more blemished in reality than in our historical myths, but we can conceive of their existence nonetheless.

Not so the modern hero. Who really believes that some lone off-duty cop will defeat a pack of terrorists? Who believes that the next U.S. President will be able to fight like Batman? These new stories are what might be termed *postmodern*—they are pure play within a given form. As in a video game, the villains have no souls, and neither do the heroes. The genre has become disconnected from its original roots in our historical past and from ordinary human behavior.

But this does not mean that nothing is to be learned from such films. Two conclusions can be quickly drawn. Either we are culturally experiencing what has been termed the "Clinton Effect," a large-scale moral disillusionment that has the majority of Americans believing that heroes in fact no longer exist (i.e., everyone is doing "it"); or we are in a posture in which the only plausible leader will have to be "bigger than life"—a very frightening prospect. It might be noted on this latter point that a film theorist named Siegfried Kracauer argued something very similar from his observations about German cinema prior to the rise of Hitler. Kracauer argued specifically that the popularity of historical spectacles in Germany in the 1920s tended to show history as playing out individual passions and psychoses more than the unfolding of social, economic, and political events and movements. Germany had thus become obsessed with the cult of the giant, Romantic individual. Those films bore an eerie similarity to the current state of American film.

How should the Christian respond? First, by remembering that we follow a hero who is indeed larger than life, our Lord Jesus Christ. We cannot allow Jesus to be reduced by arrogant theologians who want to decide what He could and could not have done or said. This battle must be fought with all energy. The integrity of the Scriptures and the truth about the Lord Jesus, passed down to us by courageous women and men who lived their faith at great cost, is the only antidote to our cultural problems. Second, we must see to it that we live out lives in this world that are above reproach. The church must emphasize holy discipline and show through living examples the power of the Gospel. We must become heroes ourselves.

The genre that is perhaps most interesting to examine is the Hollywood romance, though ironically it tends to be the one most maligned. I can't number how many times I have heard Christians blame Hollywood's version of love for some of the problems in American society. "Hollywood teaches that love is a feeling, whereas the Bible teaches that love is an act of will. Hollywood has reduced love to sex. It is ruining our children and destroying our families."

Hollywood does, of course, teach that love is a feeling. And Hollywood does tend to punctuate all love with sex. And this *is* problematic. But the popular romances I see also suggest that love is the supreme human experience. They suggest that love is meant to last forever and that there is one man for every woman. And they suggest that love overcomes great impediments because when two people fall in love, the arrangement has been made by powers above.

The temptation is to name films here, but there would not be enough space—*Rocky, Ghost, Sleepless in Seattle, The Last of the Mohicans*, and *Titanic* top a list that would include hundreds of titles.

Take, for example, *Titanic* again. How do you save a film project with an expense ledger that is ballooning out of control? You center one of the century's great tragedies around a formula love story. Free-spirited American boy meets disillusioned beautiful girl. She tames him. He makes her come alive emotionally. All this is set before a backdrop of exotic luxury and adventure. The characters are made of cardboard, the dialogue is laughable, but it somehow strangely works. The popularity of *Titanic* made fools of all of us know-it-all critics and academics who groaned at the schmaltzy story. It forced the question, *Why* are people drawn back to these same romantic formulas again and again?

Before answering, recognize that the queen of all formulas in the world of formula fiction is the love story. She has reigned for hundreds of years. In fact, it is fair to say that the patterns have circulated in western literature since the days of the medieval troubadours. That is a few years longer than slasher films have been around. The poet Dante built elements of a love story into his grand depiction of hell, purgatory, and heaven, *The Divine Comedy*, written around the year 1300.

The pattern love story finds two diverse people led together by "fate." They fall immediately in love but face some barriers—distance, war, belligerent fathers, misunderstanding, class. In the end they unite, sometimes in the context of death (tragedy), sometimes in a marriage (comedy). From Dante to Shakespeare to Dickens to your typical Harlequin novel, this is the way the stories unfold.

Now, *why* does the formula work?

The answer is that the aroma of Christianity permeates western culture, even now in the postmodern era.

It was Christianity that explained the power of love. Scriptures teach that love between a man and woman is a gift given by God to enable us to understand God's love for us. Adam knew Eve. God foreknew His people. Christ married human flesh in the Incarnation. The people of God await a wedding feast in heaven. The "formula" love story has its roots in the Word of God. The diversity of the lovers in the formula stories recalls the differences between God and us, and the original differences between he and she, Adam and Eve. The "love at first sight" component recalls the mystery of God's attachment to us ("while we were yet sinners, Christ died for us," Romans 5:8, KJV). The impediments to the relationship recall the intrusions of sin upon the communion between God and man. The final union of the lovers recalls the promise of paradise, where we shall behold Jesus Christ face to face. Dante described heaven through the analogy of beholding his beloved Beatrice, and the church has traditionally maintained that the intimacy of marriage brings us closest to understanding divine love.

And so, what is to be made of the continuing popularity of the romance even in that great machine of popular culture, Hollywood? We can recognize in it how desperately all people long for a fellowship that transcends common human experience. People are lonely and long for permanence in love, and so they long for God, sometimes at the same time running from Him.

Take another look at *Titanic*. There are primarily three intimate moments in that film between the two lovers, Jack and Rose. The first is on the bow of the ship, where Jack holds Rose who stands on the rail with arms outspread toward the sea. The second is when Jack sketches Rose as she reclines nude on a couch. The third is when the two consummate their love physically in an antique car in the ship's cargo hold. In each scene the dynamics of the film change dramatically to emphasize the almost religious importance of these moments.

In the first of these scenes Jack (Leonardo DiCaprio) stands against the rail in the foremost part of the deck leaning out over the sea. The sun is setting, coloring the sky in brilliant amber and red hues. Behind him appears Rose (Kate Winslet), her hair blowing softly in the wind, her face lit beautifully by the sky. An airy melody begins in the sound track as Rose and Jack come together. He has her stand on the rail and close her eyes. She reaches out to the sea as he holds her. The motions of the two fall into artistic poses, the scene beginning to resemble a painting, visual poetry. Forget the dialogue at this point and just absorb the visuals. Everything about the way the scene is shot and presented, a set-piece almost apart from the rest of the story (just as they are apart from the rest of the ship's company), suggests momentary transcendence—emblematic "love." Not love in the particulars of these two extremely young people, but love in the ideal, love as that which is akin to holiness. The aura around the scene bears remarkable similarity to the manner in which transcendent moments are typically shot in "Christian films" like *Ben Hur* or *Chariots of Fire*. The visual and auditory mechanics of the film change for several moments, and the same alterations in style signal the "transcendence" in the other two intimate scenes.

One could watch this and think, "How sad that people in this world replace God with sentimental romance." True as this is, a better conclusion would be to see in such Hollywood moments an affirmation of what we Christians hold so dear; namely, that man was made for something much larger than biological existence. We are made to know intimately and to be known. Ultimately, we are made for God.

The worldview of the present age may be dominated by evolution and scientific materialism, but people all around us are crying out for something so much richer, since the stamp of the Creator remains imprinted on His creatures. We should in a sense find it heartening that the drugstore rack holds dozens of cheap romances. What a great place to begin a conversation.

CHAPTER FIVE

FILMS AND CHILDREN

❀

So much has been written over the past decade on the subject of media influences on children that it is difficult to know where to start to address the topic. Perhaps the way to begin is to restate a point made earlier. The people most responsible for what children see in films are parents. Put aunts, uncles, siblings, teachers, and concerned church elders a far distant second, and forget about looking to the industry itself or to government for significant help. Parents must help their children understand how films work, what they mean, and how they relate to our Christian faith. Let everything that follows be prefaced by this.

The first rule regarding children and film is simple: Visual sophistication is the standard by which most young people evaluate what they watch. If a film is fresh and technically sophisticated, kids are more liable to find it entertaining. Practically speaking, this means it may be hard to get your little ones to warm up immediately to *Darby O'Gill and the Little People* (1959) and *Shane* (1953). Great as those films are, they are old; and to the modern child, old is not a good thing. Most parents know this from humbling personal experience.

To a certain degree, this predisposition will fade in time as children mature toward adulthood. Several years ago I decided to treat my two young nieces, who were then twelve and ten, by inviting them over to watch a great old movie, Michael Powell's *The Red Shoes* (1948), a dark retelling of a Hans Christian Andersen fairy tale and possibly the best film ever made involving ballet. Since the girls had been studying ballet almost as long as they could walk, the film seemed a sure thing. Unfortunately, within fifteen minutes both had slumped into their chairs and had begun to weigh the heavy cost of enduring this old film with their uncle. Three years later, however, I noticed a copy of *The Red Shoes* at their mother's house. They had seen it again, this time on television, and loved it. How great a change a few years can make in the life of a child!

However, not all prejudices wear off this easily. Many young people hold firmly to the belief that older black-and-white films or silent films are by their very nature inferior to current releases. If the moviemakers had known how to do color or sound, the thinking goes, they could have made better films. Many of these young people enter adulthood with the same belief and so brush aside some of the finest films ever made on their way to the New Releases shelf for some twice-chewed and gratuitous bit of pop cultural stew.

One flaw in the logic is that in many films black-and-white was a careful choice instead of color. *Manhattan, Raging Bull,* and *Schindler's List* are three of the more celebrated films of the last three decades, and all three were made black-and-white in an era of color. Many people are unaware of the fact that the first three-color film, Rouben Mamoulian's retelling of Thackeray's *Vanity Fair*, was made in 1935. It is likewise instructive that Charlie Chaplin made, arguably, his two greatest silent films in the era of sound, *City Lights* (1931) and *Modern Times* (1936).

Nevertheless, logic and film history aside, tell the average young person that the film you plan on showing them is black-and-white or silent and they will assume that you have no concept of quality. The opposite is true, however, for the greatest measure of the quality of art is the test of time, and younger viewers have little historical or artistic context with which to evaluate what they see. Most kids, therefore, evaluate art on a purely emotional level or with the aesthetic standards of the present culture—the latest fads. Ask a younger person to name their favorite film, and nine times out of ten they will name a film that will be forgotten in five years.

It is interesting that the problem described above is less likely to occur with children and books because literature is not technology-dependent like film. *Charlotte's Web* or *Black Beauty* or any Beatrix Potter tale reads just as well now as when first written. Pass one along to a child in a shiny new binding, and they will not even know it is "old." Not so with older films.

It may be that this noticeable prejudice of young people against older films contributed to the first important wave of film criticism, led by Andre Bazin of France in the 1950s, who argued that a technology-based medium like film must always evolve toward greater and greater representations of reality and should therefore be evaluated on this basis. A film shot on location in Wales is on some level superior to one shot in a back lot of a Hollywood studio dressed up to look like a Welsh town, even when that film is as great as John Ford's *How Green Was My Valley* (1941). At least, this is the argument, and common experience seems to back it up. Modern films, the better ones, are indeed much more dynamic *visually* than films of the past. A great old adventure film like *Gunga Din* (1939) still amuses and entertains the film buffs and old duffers of this culture, but few Gen X-ers will choose it over the newest Hollywood thriller, though the latter is ever so predictable. The reason is visual excitement. A young person raised on the vivid imagery and rapid editing pace of video games and MTV will find an older adventure film like *Gunga Din* both slow and technically primitive.

It is a fact that the films that tend to date most quickly are those that depend for their success on purely technical merits—like action or sci-fi films. Seen *Forbidden Planet* lately? Or even the first *Star Trek* movies?

Children don't have to read Andre Bazin's essays to understand that technical merit is a prominent part of the visual pleasure of the cinema. To many fans of the original *Star Wars* films, particularly the first two, the long-awaited prequel, *The Phantom Menace*, was a bit of a letdown. The story line lacked freshness, the characters were flat, and the suspense was minimal. Yet, for children who did not see those earlier films or who only saw them as relics of the past, *The Phantom Menace* was a great success. Children recognized the technical excellence of the film and valued that over the weaker narrative elements. After all, the light saber of Darth-Mal is superior to the one wielded by Darth Vader.

The challenge for parents is to acknowledge the child's sense of what is visually interesting, while at the same time helping that child develop the ability to enjoy what was interesting in the past. This can only be accomplished, however, if we get past our own prejudices and make the effort to sympathize with our children's experience.

An older movie, say *Citizen Kane* (1941, often called the greatest American film), requires more mental effort for young people to watch and understand simply because it speaks in a somewhat different visual language than many contemporary films. Thus, watching the film, if you are unprepared, can produce a certain measure of fatigue. This is a physiological reality that can be best understood through a couple of analogies. Consider how difficult it is to see a foreign film when you have not seen many. First, you have to read subtitles, some of which are long and hard to make out. Then you have to think through the different cultural attitudes that shape the story and the techniques of filmmaking. Then you have to deal with unfamiliar actors and actresses. All of these challenges require mental effort not required when you watch the latest Blockbuster favorite. For another example, consider the difficulty of encountering opera for the first time. Many adults cringe at the thought of sitting through an opera simply because they know so little about its language, history, and rules, and therefore they know how difficult that first performance will be to digest. So it is with older films and younger viewers. The quirky camera angles, heavy use of shadow, and fragmented narrative of *Citizen Kane* will puzzle and frustrate most younger viewers trained in a different type of film experience.

Black-and-white films operate in a different visual mode than do color films, which is, by the way, why so many film purists decried colorization when Ted Turner tried to popularize it on his network. Great black-and-white films like *Citizen Kane* or *It's a Wonderful* Life or *To Kill a Mockingbird* were made to be black-and-white. Their visual compositions depend more heavily on shadowing and gradations of light than do most color films. Colorize the opening shots of the looming Gothic mansion of Xanadu from *Citizen Kane* and those shots will lose their emotional force. Similarly the nostalgia of Frank Capra's small-town America in *It's a Wonderful Life* or novelist Harper Lee's Maycomb, Alabama, in Robert Mulligan's masterful *To Kill a*

The gritty texture of the Alabama courtroom in Robert Mulligan's *To Kill a Mockingbird* (1962) is best expressed through black-and-white film.

Mockingbird seeps through the grainy black-and-white textures of those classics much more effectively *because* they lack color.

Children need to be introduced to older black-and-white film, or even to silent film, incrementally, just as a young adult needs to be slowly introduced to Chaucer's Middle English in *The Canterbury Tales*. It is prudent, for example, to start a child off with an older film that has a guaranteed appeal like *The Wizard of Oz* or *Old Yeller* before moving on to less accessible classics like *The Biscuit Eater* (1940). Taste in all matters must be cultivated after all, unless we are comfortable with our children thinking dinner at McDonald's followed by Disney's *Tarzan* is as good as it gets.

The second major point to be made on the subject of young people and film regards the effects of film violence on children. In an age when most kids think Pokemon is cute, parents need to understand how children experience what they see on the screen.

Numerous studies have been conducted showing how film and television violence affects children, and although the results vary, a general consensus holds that too much negative imagery can lead to aberrant behavior. Nothing surprising here, except perhaps the amount of money that researchers have spent proving what every parent knows—consider the basic parental instinct to cover the eyes of a child to prevent the sight of blood or death. One of the most affecting literary devices and an old one, for instance, is to allow a child to narrate or participate firsthand in a great tragedy. Mark Twain showed this in *Huckleberry Finn*, the great nineteenth-century novel narrated by the boy Huck. There is something unusually chilling about Huck's description of his Pap's attempts to kill him with a knife when in a drunken rage; just because the horror is described by a boy it lingers in the memory. Several films have exploited this method as well—three of them classics, *The 400 Blows, The Tin Drum,* and *Schindler's List.*

One of the unique aspects of film that gets discussed rather little outside of film classes is the voyeuristic appeal of the cinema—which is to say, that quality of film that puts us in the role of the Peeping Tom. We derive a certain pleasure when watching films in the conscious or unconscious knowledge that we are invading the private space of the characters on the screen. The room is dark, and the images are large, and we can leave the theater in complete anonymity. We watch things on a movie screen we would blush to catch a glimpse of in real life.

The filmmaker who understood this principle better than any other was Alfred Hitchcock, and he explored it in several films including *Vertigo, Rear Window,* and *Psycho.* In the latter film, Norman Bates looks through a peephole at Janet Leigh who is undressing for a shower just before he leaves to change identities and murder her. Hitchcock allows us to share Norman Bates's point of view through the peephole so that we become complicit in some sense in the crime committed against her. We are encouraged to desire her, and then we violate and are violated with her. The shower scene from *Psycho* is one of the most recognized scenes in any film ever made, because it is so frightening; and the fright is in the way Hitchcock plays off our voyeuristic posture as film watchers.

The primary reason why film places us in such an alluring and yet vulnerable position is that the symbols we are following on screen look like the things they represent. In other words, the characters being played are not conjured in our imagination as in poetry or a novel or in a painting; they are conjured by images of real people, as with the theater. However, in theater the artifice is apparent. We see the limitations of the set and the textures of costume and makeup. Not usually in film. In film there is seeming reality. The type of symbolism inherent in film is called iconic. Things are represented by other things like them. James Stewart stands for Jefferson Smith, Humphrey Bogart stands for Rick Blaine, Meryl Streep stands for Karen Blixen. These symbols compel us and convince us by their nature.

For adults the line between reality and fiction is, seemingly, easily drawn, although even adults often think of actors as the roles they play rather than the people they are. Most film actors resist this confusion and insist they are simply artists, not to be confused with the roles they play. However, there have been those who made hay with the fact that they could take their screen roles into the real world. Consider, for example, Marilyn Monroe and Jayne Mansfield. Monroe used her screen persona to create a cultural phenomenon, although even she wanted to move away from it and do "serious" films toward the end of her career. Mansfield, on the other hand, would walk her dog through downtown Los Angeles wearing a scant bikini. I suppose the closest we have to that in recent times is Michael Jackson, although he isn't a film star.

Most adults, despite entertainment magazine hype and a variety of oddball anecdotes, are sensible enough to know that Anthony Hopkins is not a cannibalizing murderer and that Meg Ryan is not the perfect woman. They are merely people playing people who are those things. And yet, on the other hand, the tendency even among sensible adults is to make value judgments about actors based on the roles they play. "I can't stand ———." Fill in the blank with Hugh Grant or Sharon Stone or Meryl Streep or whomever. "I love ———." Tom Hanks, Harrison Ford, Cameron Diaz, Glenn Close, or whomever. Most of us, when we say such things, are not speaking about the quality of these performers' acting. We are speaking about the real people based on the roles they play. So perhaps we aren't so sensible after all.

Imagine the confusion that children face, and I am going to appeal to common sense here rather than the theories of child development of Piaget or other psychologists. The average child cannot imagine a real person sweating inside a Barney suit. The average child expects that Mister Rogers is always Mister Rogers, even when the camera is not rolling. Mayberry was a real place when I was a boy, and Andy Taylor, Helen Crump, Barney Fife, Floyd, and Otis were real people. I can still remember my sadness when Barney Fife left the show to move to the big city. It seemed to me that someone most certainly could have talked him out of it. While George Reeves starred as Superman on television in the fifties, he lived out a high-profile Hollywood love affair; yet the tabloids back then refused to print the story and dash the dreams of millions of children. (How times have changed!)

A child does not discriminate as an adult does between the play and the reality behind the play. The play is the reality. A child will, for example, have difficulty watching two versions of a particular film or two actors playing a certain role. At Christmastime most adults still carry the childhood tendency to watch either the Reginald Owens *Christmas Carol* or the Alistair Sim *Christmas Carol*, not both. There can only be one Heidi—Shirley Temple.

From this we can conclude what many psychologists have concluded: Children are far less able to witness screen violence as a distant fiction than are adults. The carryover into the real world is much more pronounced. Think of the child's tendency to play out Batman punches and Bruce Lee kicks after the viewing of a movie with this kind of violence. The acting out of various strains of ritualized violence in a film creates a psychological disturbance in even the "normal" child. Either he will be *more inclined* to strike out in the real world when tensions arise there, or, perhaps worse, he will distance his emotions to the point where violence no longer affects him (one explanation for the increased brutality of teens who commit crimes is their absence of grief at the sight of human suffering). Studies have shown that these consequences are most apparent with "troubled" kids. The psychological realities of the film-viewing experience in general would lead us to conclude that even if the effects in the "normal" child do not manifest themselves in overt ways, they still exist in some measure.

The third point to be made regarding children and film concerns how well or poorly children are able to detect the world-view of a particular film. Since technical matters have such an overwhelming effect on younger viewers, it is reasonable to conclude that the "message" underlying many films often gets lost on younger viewers. There is more to the subject than this, however.

A child assumes a basic integrity and truthfulness in the message of a film. Why should a film lie when it looks so real and entertains so well? Beyond this, why would one film be truthful or worthwhile while another, that looks just the same, not be? Think about Disney films in this context. When a child has seen *Bambi* and *Dumbo* and *Snow White and the Seven Dwarfs*, he learns to recognize certain traits of Disney films—their artistic originality, their celebration of little or unlikely heroes, and their tendency to pit good versus evil in head-on fashion, to name three. Those deductions become assumptions when that child sees future Disney films. It is assumed that *Pocahontas* and *Aladdin* and *Mulan* share the same qualities as the former films. The child watches with the same confident eyes, unprepared to make any discriminations about the nature of the content. So the child learns that John Smith was a handsome and heroic savior when in actuality he was a short, red-faced mercenary with a talent for enlarging stories. The child learns that a kiss on the first date, the magic carpet ride for Aladdin and Jasmine, is appropriate. And the child learns that traditional gender roles are highly suspect—a girl, Mulan, can certainly be every bit as much a soldier as a man.

We actually performed a little experiment for this chapter, showing the film *Mulan* to a group of ten young children and then asking for their impressions. Most of the kids, from good Christian homes, were savvy enough to know that crickets can't talk and that dead ancestors can't either, but none questioned the film's assumption that women could be great warriors if given the chance and that people can do anything they put their minds to. So, in other words, these Christian children walked away from the film having been reinforced in two tenets of modern humanism—gender roles are primarily cultural, and self-esteem is a function of positive thinking.

To take a slightly different approach, how many children will wonder why there are no major black characters in the newer Disney film *Tarzan*, which supposedly is set in Africa? Adults may pick this up, but the thought will not likely occur to a child.

The point here is that children embrace the larger assumptions of the films they see because the films have so strong a flavor of actuality, and they lack the ability to filter out the errors in those assumptions. No doubt this is one reason why so many young people suffer with problems of self-worth, having unconsciously developed the notion from films (and television) that physical beauty and sexual desirability is the major component of a young person's value. I cannot think of many films that say this outright, but nearly every pop film radiates this message through its frames to the many young people who watch. Similarly, the culture of victimization that has been bred in modern America, particularly among the young, is in part a function of the largely idealized worlds that films create, worlds that make our poor sinful one at times seem rather lackluster.

So, a child needs help learning to think critically about what he or she watches. There was a time when parents could assume the average film made for children would not undercut Christian ethics. Certainly this is no longer true. Parents must commit to watching films with their children and talking about them. If parents neglect this task, they can expect problems as their children act out the ideology they have assumed from what they have been allowed to see.

After we showed *Mulan* to our gathering of children, we found that although the kids had picked up the humanistic messages of the film, they were nevertheless eager to find ways to apply their understanding of Christianity to the film. They grasped quickly the idea that an unlikely hero like Mulan is in some ways similar to the heroes in the Bible—David, Daniel, Gideon. This allowed us to explain how God used a very unlikely method to save the world through His Son, Jesus Christ, and prepared His people for Jesus' coming through these older heroes. We also found that the children quickly rejected the notion of getting help from ancestors when reminded of the power of God available through prayer. Also, the kids were able to personalize Mulan's challenges in a Christian way by concluding that in the Christian fight, God strengthens and helps His servants as they engage the enemy courageously.

All of this discussion took less than twenty minutes and was enthusiastically received by the kids. They rather liked the honor of being asked their opinions, as well as the thrill of putting together what they know of their faith with their daily experiences. They also were offered a way to make two seemingly disparate messages coherent, the message of *Mulan* and the truth of the Gospel.

The importance of such debriefings can hardly be overestimated. One of the major cultural shifts in my lifetime affecting children came with the introduction of videos and new marketing strategies for films aimed at children. When I was a boy, I didn't suffer on the playground for not having seen *The Sound of Music* or *Mary Poppins*. When my friends referred to these films, I shifted the subject to hockey or baseball or my favorite television show. Nowadays, however, kids are much more conscious of the need to keep up with movie culture. It wasn't even enough to see *Tarzan* or *The Phantom Menace* recently; children had to see them within the first couple weeks of release. With the large-scale marketing of these films, which is virtually inescapable, children feel tremendous peer pressure to keep up with the latest pop cultural rage. Christian parents can either try to shield their children from all of this by removing the television, avoiding Blockbuster, and not taking their kids to the store, or they can learn to use the messages of the culture as opportunities for instruction in the truth. I think the latter is the better strategy, although I have great respect for parents who have succeeded in raising happy kids apart from television and mass culture.

We have to always remember how Paul used the words of Greek poets in Acts 17 as a method of creating a point of contact for the presentation of the Gospel to those gathered at Mars Hill. "For in Him we live and move and exist, as even some of your own poets have said, 'For we also are His children'" (v. 28, NASB). Paul is quoting Aratus and is also suggesting the words of Cleanthes in his "Hymn to Zeus," of all things, as a means of opening a door to communication. Paul was translating the Gospel into the language of that particular culture. Remember that Paul urges this kind of aggressive Christianity in his personal defense to the Corinthian Christians who questioned his motives: "To the Jews I became as a Jew, that I might win Jews; to those who are under the Law, as under the Law . . . that I might win those who are under the Law. . . . I have become all things to all men, that I may by all means save some" (1 Corinthians 9:20, 22, NASB).

Now we may not be "saving" our children in the evangelistic sense that Paul intended in these words, but we will be helping our children think as aggressive Christians if we teach them how to understand film. And we will be giving them the tools to evangelize others.

To parents who feel this kind of approach is too heavy a burden—are we to see all the films and shows our children watch and then find time to talk about them?—a visit back to the sixth chapter of Deuteronomy might be in order, for there the Lord commands His people to teach the Scriptures "diligently to your sons and . . . talk of them when you sit in your house and when you walk by the way and when you lie down and when you rise up" (Deut. 6:7, NASB). The intent here was certainly not to have a Bible study three or four times a day, but to refer every life situation back to the Word of God throughout the day. Children need Bible memorization and study, and they also need to be reinforced over and over again in how God's Word teaches us to understand the world.

My food satisfies me in the morning. I learn to thank God for this food and recall how He promises to meet my daily needs. I see a lovely sky and am reminded that the heavens declare God's glory. I hurt myself or have my feelings hurt and am reminded of the effects of sin and the hope of a perfect heaven. I watch a movie and learn of how fallen men are led to think and act and what consequences come of those thoughts and actions. It is the responsibility of parents to see that children understand the world in this way.

A thoughtful parent will respond to different films differently. From time to time that parent will be obliged to say no. At other times the comment may need to be, "Perhaps in a few years." A parent who cares about the Word of God and his or her children will pray for wisdom from God who alone gives wisdom. That parent will try to make informed decisions, and sometimes that parent will make mistakes. But the task of seeking in all ways to teach a child how to love and serve God is never a mistake.

CHAPTER SIX

LITURGICAL PATTERNS IN FILM

🌀

An interesting approach to the question of how Christianity has influenced film is to consider how the film industry has borrowed from the church the tools for conveying the divine, which is a stuffy way of saying that when filmmakers originally wanted to make movies with "religious" qualities they went to church to find out how. Let me offer an illustration.[1]

In the crucial sequence of Rouben Mamoulian's 1934 film *We Live Again*, a young Russian nobleman named Nekhludov (Fredric March), overcome by guilt at having debauched and then deserted a young peasant girl, Katusha (Anna Sten), enters his private room and shuts the door. At this moment the straightforward narrative in the film abruptly stops. What follows is a symbolic montage of cinematic gestures that conveys what is happening in Nekhludov's soul. He crosses the room to a piano, where he sits and begins to play a doleful hymn. This shot dissolves into an image of a church interior during a Mass, and then back to Nekhludov whose head is tilted back in emotion. He rises from the piano and walks to a mantel on which sits an icon. The hymn played on the piano is carried on the sound track, increasing in volume as he draws nearer the icon. With a gesture of despair Nekhludov bows before this altar and prays that he might "live again."

After this scene the narrative continues as before, but the main character is now a changed man—merciful, sacrificial, and heroic. The frozen moment in the private room allows for a complete reshuffling of character behavior and narrative expectation. It also does something remarkable for the film viewer— it invites the viewer to participate in the religious awakening being displayed. Since we have been drawn by the camera to identify with this character, we are also drawn to achieve the same elevation of soul.

If you examine this scene carefully, or any number of the hundred similar scenes in a hundred similar films, you can't help but notice the sacramental qualities of it. Nekhludov's "inner room" experience is a kind of incarnation. God has entered his life, and Mamoulian, the filmmaker, has had to resort to symbolic film gestures—the hymn, the icon, the church dissolve, the posturing—to convey this. The gestures run counter to anything else in the film in order to alert viewers to the sacredness of what is being conveyed. It is rather like the robes, incense, choreographed movements, and iconography associated with communion liturgies. The spiritual realm has broken through the physical in order to redeem it.

Liturgical moments such as this one occur in a wide range of films, from the overtly Christian to the quasi-religious. The key features are the incarnational gestures that intrude suddenly upon a narrative in order to redeem it. In fact, the Christian qualities of *We Live Again* are rather ambiguous in the final analysis. The story of this film derives from Leo Tolstoy's Christian novel *Resurrection*. Tolstoy's Nekhludov, however, will not approach conversion until he has joined himself to the peasant girl,

The visual style is transformed in Rouben Mamoulian's *We Live Again* (1934) once God has entered Nekhludov's life. This image from the film illustrates a "sacramental" moment.

Katusha, and suffered degradation with her as she is imprisoned for prostitution. He comes to realize the futility of life without God and in desperation begins to read the Scriptures. This occurs at the very end of the book. Mamoulian places the conversion much earlier, nearer the initial encounter between the nobleman and the ruined peasant girl, and compresses the conversion process into the emotional scene described. This throws into question the impetus for the man's conversion—is it a sense of sin and helplessness, or is it because of "the woman"? Whichever way the film is read, be it the pull of God or the pull of romantic love, Nekhludov is reborn and the film narrative restructured.

Since the entrance of God cannot be shown in a film literally, it must be evoked metaphorically. (Again think in terms of sacramental rituals.) The best way to do this is usually to change suddenly the techniques the filmmaker has employed previously. In a film of heavy shadows, a sudden burst of light might work, for instance. In a film of frenetic activity, a set of static shots might work. There are certain clichés that Hollywood occasionally falls back on—like the old angelic choir of biblical epics or violins played in a minor key—but the technique has been employed with great variety throughout film history.

A dramatic example can be found in an explicitly Christian film made in 1970 by Gateway Films called *The Cross and the Switchblade*, based ostensibly on the spiritual autobiography of David Wilkerson, the rural minister whose outreach to gangs and drug addicts in New York City led to the founding of Teen Challenge, a remarkably successful Christian halfway house network. The film loosely adapts Wilkerson's book of the same name.

Whereas the book concerns itself with the expansiveness of the ministry, the film narrows the focus to one incident in Wilkerson's early ministry that gave him an early sign of potential success. This was the conversion of one of the warlords of a New York gang, Nicki Cruz. The narrow focus serves to make the story more filmable, but it also allows director Don Murray to steer the objective account of Wilkerson's ministry toward a single "incarnational moment," not unlike that of Mamoulian's *We Live Again*. This will be a sermon delivered by Wilkerson that prompts the change in Cruz. The sermon functions also as direct address to the film viewers, calling them likewise to repentance.

With Pat Boone playing David Wilkerson and Erik Estrada playing Cruz, the film narrative is structured like Francis Thompson's "Hound of Heaven," with Wilkerson pursuing Cruz through back alleys and tenements and telling him over and over again of God's love. Cruz largely resists, but a developing pattern of facial closeups suggests that his defenses are steadily weakening. In the climactic scene, Wilkerson gathers two rival gangs into a theater for a youth rally and, after quieting the crowd, begins the sermon that wins over Cruz.

The pattern of closeups that has developed to this point becomes more prominent as quick cuts among the various gang members keep coming back to Cruz. Wilkerson's sermon reaches a crescendo of emotion with the words, "Open up your heart and let all that bitterness run out, and let Jesus Christ come in." Just then the frame freezes. Boone's voice is echoed through a synthesizer and behind his image an artificial streak of blue light extends diagonally. A bell begins to ring softly. The device continues for ten full seconds, after which the narrative resumes, the sound track carrying, however, a chorus that sings, "God loves you, God loves Nicki Cruz." When the camera cuts back to Cruz, his eyes are full of tears of conviction. He is a changed man. From this moment in the narrative, his entire character moves differently. He now loves Wilkerson as well as God and works to bring peace where there had been gang strife. Thus, the "message" becomes a kind of sacrament as God becomes enfleshed in Cruz, the metaphoric cinematic cues suggesting the miracle.

Although clumsily performed in *The Cross and the Switchblade*, this "sacramental style" of filmmaking is quite effective and, as I have suggested, pervasive. Examine the key moments of the great biblical epics like *Ben Hur*, *The Ten Commandments*, and *The Robe* and you will find it. These tend to be the memorable scenes—Ben Hur finding his sister and mother cleansed from leprosy, the Red Sea parting, etc. Filmmakers working with religious material tend to build toward that one key moment, just as a worship service slowly builds, and when the moment comes, all bets are off. The style is not unlike what you find in Hollywood musicals like *The Wizard of Oz* in which the world is transformed to colorful lyricism once the music begins to play. And the devices are not limited to religiously explicit films; you find them in *On the*

Waterfront, Babette's Feast, Gallipoli, Taxi Driver, Open City, and a wide range of films from all countries—some serious independent films like *Pickpocket* (Robert Bresson, 1959) and others bits of light Hollywood fluff like *Titanic*.

As the incarnation becomes the central metaphor in many films of this type, so also the ritual of the Passion becomes a story pattern. It is, after all, the suffering and death of Jesus the Savior that completes the redemptive act begun in Bethlehem. Christianity has become such a part of western thinking that when films have even the slightest hint of Christianity in them, you often find an allusion to the suffering of Christ.

The pattern usually becomes part of the plight of the main character, which can be as diverse as that of Nicholas Cage in *Bringing out the Dead* (1999), Sylvester Stallone in *Rocky* (1976), Gary Cooper in *Meet John Doe* (1941), or Jennifer Jones in *The Song of Bernadette* (1943). These characters and many others like them undergo a holy pilgrimage toward suffering that ultimately redeems them and the communities they represent. For example, in *Rocky* the pummeling that Rocky Balboa receives from Apollo Creed is necessary to give him validity as a worthwhile individual in his own eyes and in those of his girlfriend, Adrian; yet it also vicariously regenerates the many down-and-out Philadelphians who stake their hopes on this nobody's title chance. The crosscuts to Rocky's city pals in the stands during the fight enforce this. Likewise in *The Song of Bernadette*, Bernadette's perseverance in the face of skepticism validates her "divine call" and carries along the many broken men and women who stream to Lourdes in the film in the hope of a divine touch.

Often these characters undergo a long purgative ritual before the climactic moments of sacrifice. The ritual includes physical, emotional, and spiritual suffering and typically ends only when the character reaches a point of resignation. In Frank Borzage's 1932 retelling of the Hemingway novel *A Farewell to Arms*, Gary Cooper as Frederick Henry deserts the army and makes a long and dangerous trek across war-torn Europe to reach the woman he loves, who is pregnant and dying. Borzage makes numerous visual references to the Cross throughout the long montage that tells the story of the journey. Likewise, Father LaForgue in *Black Robe* loses all his companions as he continues upriver to the Indian mission where he is called to serve. He is betrayed by his closest friend, tempted sexually and psychologically, tortured, and consistently misunderstood. In the Borzage film, Henry resigns himself finally at Catherine's deathbed, lifting her from it to an open window outside which church bells ring out the armistice. In *Black Robe*, Father LaForgue accepts the miserable circumstances at the Huron mission and the certain failure of the mission; yet he vows to love and serve the Indians until death, serving them Communion in a small hut that rests in the shadow of a large cross.

Passion narratives in film are remarkably common in part because they are built into the long tradition of heroism in western literature that grows out of medieval stories of warrior heroes. The patterns pass unmistakenly from *Beowulf*, *Le Morte D'Arthur*, and *Sir Gawain and the Green Knight* to Shakespeare and Spenser to Dickens and Tennyson to the mass-produced popular literature of the twentieth century. The historical and literary tradition is hard to shake, even in postmodern America. Thus, in vehicles as seemingly devoid of Christian influence as *The Karate Kid* (1984), *The Terminator* (1984), *Batman* (1989), and *Unforgiven* (1992) we find echoes of the same heroic stories grounded in the primary Christian model of redemption, the Passion.

One expects to find some threads of real Christianity still

dangling on the shirts of those who make films like this, and, yes, they are often there. Martin Scorsese, for instance, whose films all follow dark pilgrimages, considered the priesthood as a young man. Pier Paolo Pasolini, an avowed Marxist who made the most eloquent Jesus film to date, *The Gospel According to St. Matthew* (1966), had just completed a reading of the Gospels during a papal visit to a local town. Elia Kazan was inspired to make *On the Waterfront* by an account of a Catholic priest who came to the aid of longshoremen in a corrupt New Jersey union. Yet, enough Christianity still perfumes our culture and literature that films with these patterns seem at times just to happen, like *Forrest Gump* or *Babette's Feast*.

The Christian faith has powerfully impacted every sphere of art in the West. At the same time that the church cautions filmmakers and the general public about the potential corrosiveness of film on our culture, films emerge that will remain as masterpieces of Christian art for the next hundred years. What this suggests above everything else is the abiding power of the Christian faith, which seems to always find a voice, irregardless of place, time, or medium.

An illustration of one such work would be the wonderful Danish film *Babette's Feast* (1987). Although the context of the film is the plight of two poor daughters of an austere sectarian minister, the story itself is more directed to the power of art to uplift and reconcile; yet one cannot watch *Babette's Feast* without a profound sense that the power of the film is more a function of the infiltration of Christianity onto the subject of art. In other words, it is a film about art that gets taken over by the Christianity that is the story's context.

The success of *Babette's Feast* in the international film market (it won the Academy Award for best foreign film in 1987 as well as a host of other awards) suggests the power of its subject.

Perhaps no other foreign film has developed as high a reputation in America until Roberto Benigni's brilliant *Life Is Beautiful* in 1998.

Director Gabriel Axel took the story from one of Isak Dinesen's most successful short stories. Dinesen came to the material in an odd way. She had just returned from an expensive Venetian holiday with friends in 1949 out of money and so decided to try her hand publishing in the lucrative market of American women's magazines. A friend wagered that she could not be published in the *Saturday Evening Post* because of her style, and in reply she asked what the American public liked to read. Her friend, Geoffrey Gorer, told her, "Write about food. Americans are obsessed with food." So she wrote "Babette's Feast," only to have the *Post* reject it. Fortunately for the world, the *Ladies' Home Journal* picked it up in 1950. Dinesen eventually incorporated it in her collection *Anecdotes of Destiny*, published in 1953.

Gabriel Axel made only a few modifications in adapting the story for film. The location was changed from Norway to the Jutland coast in Denmark, Axel's homeland. This allowed for changes in Dinesen's setting—adding "grey, yellow, pink, and other colours" to the film's drab white-gray houses and muted sky. The added austerity allows for the rich visual contrasts Axel builds around. The principal characters of Babette and General Lorens Lowenhielm are also subtly altered. Babette, played by the graceful Stephane Audran, has more soulfulness in the film. Lowenhielm is likewise more of a melancholy romantic.

The story centers on Babette, a refugee cook and artist, but begins with two sisters, Martine and Filippa, the repressed yet dutiful daughters of a pietist Lutheran minister who has founded a sect of believers on the Jutland coast. A voice-over narration begins their story and takes them from beautiful youth to a lonely age, when Babette will enter their lives. The sisters have each been loved seriously once but were discouraged by their father, who "was well-respected, and perhaps also a little feared." His ascetic doctrines and paternal selfishness have seemingly barred his daughters from life's principal joys.

The young Martine is courted by a handsome lieutenant of the hussars, Lorens Lowenhielm, a somewhat dissolute officer sent as punishment to the Jutland by his commanding officer to stay with his pious aunt, a disciple of the minister. There he meets and falls in love with Martine, only to find a cold welcome at the minister's home. After failing to break the girl free from these pious rigors, he rides off, vowing to live a full life of plea-sure and worldly success. He will eventually play court to a lady-in-waiting and advance his career brilliantly.

Filippa is courted by a world-weary Parisian opera star, Achille Papin (played by the popular French singer, Jean-Philippe Lafont), who goes on retreat in the Jutland to revital-ize his spirits. Hearing Filippa's singing in the local church, he concludes that she can be a diva and offers private lessons. When they begin rehearsing love duets from Mozart, the minister inclines her to cancel the sessions, which she does, sending a despairing Papin back to Paris.

The action is taken up years later. The minister is long dead, and the sisters, both spinsters, care for the dwindling and aging congregation, which suffers from bickering among its remain-ing members. On a stormy night in 1871, the mysterious refugee Babette arrives by boat with a letter of introduction from no less than Achille Papin, who requests that the sisters take in the woman, who, he adds, "can cook." So Babette becomes a ser-vant of Martine and Filippa, helping them manage their frugal household, assisting in certain charitable acts, and cooking their bland meals.

Fourteen years pass in this way when news comes suddenly from Paris that Babette has won a lottery of 10,000 francs. She asks the sisters' permission to cook a genuine French dinner in honor of the centenary of the minister's birth. And she does. The meal exceeds the wildest dreams of the congregational members who attend and of the one visitor from outside the community, the now General Lorens Lowenhielm, who has come in part to see if his worldly successes can stand a final test. All who eat this meal prepared by Babette are put in rapture. Old quarrels among the congregants are resolved at the table. The sisters find comfort in the knowledge that their father's work has indeed proven fruitful. And the general comes to realize that with God "all things are possible," for he has found that in choosing to turn from Martine so long before to pursue a different life, he has not lost her love in the end.

After the meal the sisters thank Babette, assuming that she will now return to Paris with her "riches," only to learn that Babette spent the entire 10,000 francs on the meal. She had formerly been the greatest chef in France, the head of the Café Anglais in Paris, where a meal serving so many would indeed cost so much, and she had offered this gift to the sisters as an artist who desires only the opportunity to do her best. In the final moment, Filippa embraces Babette and reminds her that this life is not the end, for in heaven Babette will delight the angels with her gifts. It is, of course, the lesson that Filippa, the lost diva, has learned herself.

In Dinesen's original story, Babette's sacrifice spells the ironic triumph of art in a life of incongruity. At the meal the general quotes Scripture, proclaiming that "righteousness and bliss" and "mercy and truth" have kissed, his response to the ending that this return to the minister's table has provided. But what has caused this tidy resolution is Babette's art, her cooking. It has reconciled the stiff pietism of the minister and the worldly disillusionment of the general. All meet at the table of the artist and find temporary respite. Even Achille Papin, who has led Babette to the sisters, is returned indirectly to his lost Filippa and granted "mercy." Upper-class and lower-class, experienced and naive, old and young, the disheartened and the zealous meet together and kiss.

Babette, who facilitates these closures in Dinesen's story, remains impassive to the end, declaring herself "a great artist" who willingly lost her family in the Paris uprising that brought her to the sanctuary of the village. Little attention in the short story is given to her emotional and psychological development, as Dinesen in the attitude of a Maupassant or Chekhov pulls instead on the cord of irony that laces her plot. In fact, if the original tale has a flaw, it is in the lack of depth of the central character.

With the film, however, things change, thanks to the wonders of the iconic qualities of this visual art. The changes begin with the presence of Babette herself. It is her eyes that see the sisters, her hands that prepare the dishes, her face that responds to what she has made. And these are the eyes and hands and the face of Stephane Audran, one of Europe's more graceful film beauties. She dominates every composition she enters with her warm and dignified bearing and thus adds a richness and sensitivity to the story that wasn't present on the printed page. Instead of cool irony, the film presents gracefulness and human love as the source of all reconciliations, and this seems to flavor all other aspects of the composition, creating a much stronger and more Christian texture to the work, perhaps even more than Dinesen imagined.

The alteration in tone becomes apparent in the very first moments of Babette's appearance in the sisters' home. With the rain still on her cloak from her sea journey and tears of loss in her eyes, she sits, the refugee, before Martine and Filippa in the glow of a lamp and listens as Achille Papin's letter of introduction is read. The immediate sympathy formed among the women spills over to the viewer who cannot help but form a thematic link between Babette in her loss and loneliness and the two elderly spinsters.

Axel has already prepared for this connection in telling the story of the minister's daughters earlier in the film. After the young Lowenhielm has left the minister's house for what he considers the last time, we are offered a small scene with Martine lying in her bed at night clutching a pillow. Filippa asks her if she remembers the lieutenant, and Martine responds by turning away from her, toward the camera, and saying, simply and poignantly, "Yes." Likewise, after Papin has left the minister's house for the last time, Axel provides a short commentary through a composition of the two girls sitting at the family table with the minister in the background reading his Bible. A crosscut shows Papin's boat tossing in the waves on its return to France. This image provides a graphic match with the next shot, that of Babette's boat arriving. The cook has been brought to the old women on the same waves of loss and aloneness that have carried them to their present condition.

Babette's isolation and sorrow, her passion if you will, is evoked most powerfully in one of the film's feature compositions, the one most often depicted on video boxes, a transitional sequence that allows the narration to accelerate fourteen years to the climactic events surrounding the lottery and the feast. Babette sits with a rolling brown landscape behind her, the setting sun radiating the sky; she is positioned to the right of the frame, looking off screen left. She rises gracefully, holding a small basket, and crosses left, leaving the screen to the sun-gold hills. While this little device underlines Babette's humble life in the village, it also suggests her beauty and grace, thus foreshadowing the events to come.

The physical allure of Stephane Audran as Babette draws out the visual contrasts that Axel works throughout the film. Whereas Martine and Filippa (beautifully realized by Birgitte Federspiel and Bodil Kjer) move with painful angularity, Babette moves with casual elegance. Although akin to the elderly women in her plight, her ease suggests that her exile is more free-willed. She moves in and out of the frame with easy purposefulness, particularly noticeable in compositions around the minister's table. The sisters typically sit at the end, framed symmetrically by two windows behind them. Babette never sits but instead moves in and out of the frame as she brings food. In essence, Babette is the antithesis of the minister himself, who, though dead, perpetuates his shadow, framed in oval on the sisters' wall, hovering watchfully over the latter scenes. Previously the minister had sat as a fixture at the head of the table, flanked by his girls, the members of his small sect sitting in perfect symmetry along the table sides. Whenever Babette attends the table, the symmetries are broken. At the feast, the camera circles the table to subvert any sense of compositional balance, the sisters seen then in close-up or bending to eat and drink. The windows in the background are no longer a frame. Babette has broken the spell cast by the girls' father.

Windows perform a symbolic function in the film. One of Babette's first duties upon arriving in the village is washing the windows of the house by throwing water on them from the outside, suggesting that the sisters may now look out upon the world, having emotionally repressed it before. When the sisters sit inside, framed by the windows, they look away from them. Babette looks out the windows in several key scenes. After

Babette has first learned from the women how to make their traditional ale bread, she sits alone in her small room at a table and looks out the window toward the ocean and her old, more exciting life in France; someone walks a dog outside as she watches, reinforcing the contrast. Again, shortly after this scene, the sisters are inside at the table, their place, where they encourage two members of the sect to be reconciled after a quarrel. A crosscut takes us outside where a glorious sunset lights the sky, an editing move that suggests what these Christians need to see. A montage follows—a ringing church bell, Babette at her table looking out her window, rain falling against the panes (conspicuous in their suggestion of a cross). The following scene recounts another quarrel among the sectarians, the sisters watching impotently, framed by the window in the rear. Babette enters this time with tea and rebukes the women, a foreshadowing of her later mediation.

What the windows seem most to suggest, beyond the sisters' relation to the outside world, is the presence of the distant sea, which not only isolates the village but is also the channel for the divine grace that brings redemption. Papin and Babette both travel this sea. The food for the feast comes from across the sea. When Lowenhielm toasts the women and men who eat Babette's meal, he announces a divine blessing: "Our choice is of no importance. We come to realize that mercy is infinite. We need only await it with confidence and receive it in gratitude." Infinite mercy has come to the sisters by boat—first the messenger Papin, and then the savior Babette. Although all the players make choices against their inclinations, all is restored to them in the end. Mysterious as are His ways, God is present. He watches, and He loves.

Along these lines an earlier image in the film lingers. Papin has just arrived in the village by boat and hears Filippa singing in the distance. Ironically, she sings, "God is God even if all life were ended." Papin follows the voice into the church and sits, giving thanks that God has led him to "a diva." Of course, he misses the point of the hymn, which speaks of the temporality of all worldly achievements, wanting her voice to join his own on European stages. As Filippa sings and Papin exults, the camera offers a short and telling commentary by crosscutting to the crucifix at the front of the church on which hangs a smiling Jesus. The God who oversees the plight of all these poor people, who want little more than to love and to be happy, smiles. This fleeting image explains the tone of the film perhaps better than any other.

All of these images and motifs lead inexorably to the grand finish, which is the meal itself. Axel sets this up by taking the point of view of General Lorens Lowenhielm, who, while preparing to leave for the meal, rebukes his mirror image with the words, "Vanity, vanity, all is vanity." He then addresses his younger self, imaged in a chair with arms crossed, saying, "Tonight we shall settle our score." His score is less with himself, however, than it is with the sea, the inscrutable wisdom of God, which denied to him the love of Martine so long before. The sequence continues with a cut to the sisters praying that "God's will be done," and then Babette in the kitchen preparing the pastry shells for the *Cailles en sarcophage*, which will amaze the general and lead him to offer the toast.

Babette's food blesses not only the general, but also the sisters, the sectarians, and the film viewers. It is in the scenes at the feast with Babette in the kitchen working where the visual style of the film undergoes the kind of change that I have identified as "sacramental." The kitchen with its warm brown hues and softly rising steam contrasts with all the grayness of the early parts of the film. Babette's ease of movement is likewise a contrast. And the greatest contrast is in the rich texture and color of the food itself, which gets shown repeatedly in close-ups—for example, a dessert evolving rapidly through its finishing stages as if by incantation. The only film that comes readily to mind with a similar moment is *Andrei Rublev*, Andrei Tarkovsky's loving biography of Russia's great iconographer, which explodes into color in the final images when Rublev's surviving icons are displayed on screen.

We see the results of the sacramental meal in the responses of those at the table. The general will leave peacefully after expressing to Martine that he will love her all of his remaining days until heaven unites them. The sectarians move outside and sing around a well in the center of the town under a starlit sky. "The stars have moved closer," Filippa says. Then Filippa and Martine console Babette, Filippa offering those poignant words that she will delight the angels with her artistry. The musical score of the film becomes prominent and more melodic than in the earlier scenes.

Of particular importance in the film version of Dinesen's story is the way in which Filippa's final words come as a soft rebuke to the proud French cook. Babette has said, "Throughout the world sounds one long cry from the heart of the artist, 'Give me the chance to do my very best.'" The words are an echo of something Papin had said earlier, and they come as a proud statement of her importance as an artist, as well as justification for spending 10,000 francs on one meal. Filippa's response enforces the context that Axel has developed visually throughout the film, which is that great art, like all human endeavor, is significant because it reflects the great art that is God's world and God's merciful ways. Filippa replies, sensing the pride in Babette's expression, "But this is not the end, Babette. I'm certain it's not." Both Lowenhielm and Papin had come to recognize that time diminishes all art and ambition and accomplishment. What lasts is what comes from God. Babette herself must come to this realization too.

In an interesting way, *Babette's Feast* suggests the power of the true meal of reconciliation, the Christian Eucharist. The Christian Communion meal is for remembrance of the merciful ways of God and for future promise of a greater meal when the saints will sit together around the table of Christ in paradise. In Axel's film we are left with the understanding that it is not Babette, after all, who has created the great harmonies at the end. She did not invite Papin to meet the sisters, nor did she lead Lowenhielm back to the table to find his lost Martine. Babette did not create the great echoing sea that blankets the village. She did not bring the stars to shine so brightly over the lonely people who gave their life to follow the minister, whom they felt spoke the truth of God. Babette fed the people a meal of love and a promise that confirmed their faith in the loving Lord of the universe. She used art to remind poor people of the greatest of artists, God Himself. And this marvelous little film reminds all who see it of these same truths.

Babette's Feast illustrates how the medium of film does not have to be used to debase and corrode. It can instead present to us in tangible form the goodness and mercy of God.

NOTES FOR CHAPTER 6

1. This material on the liturgical or sacramental style in film is more fully developed in Peter Fraser, *Images of the Passion: The Sacramental Mode in Film* (New York: Praeger, 1998).

CHAPTER SEVEN

THE EVOLUTION OF THE BIBLICAL SPECTACULAR

᠖

The tradition of religious film in this country is almost entirely Christian. When other religious groups appear in mainstream films, they usually become assimilated within a larger "Christian" context, ethnic and religious differences becoming part of the narrative tensions of the plot.[1] So any kind of discussion of religious film in America becomes a discussion of Christianity and film, and such a discussion inevitably swings to the subject of the biblical film or the "religious spectacular," even though such films have fallen out of favor in recent years.

The Hollywood biblical film has a history as long as American filmmaking. A version of *Quo Vadis?* was made in 1901, and as filmmakers like D. W. Griffith experimented with epic materials in the teens and twenties, traditional Christian materials became popular vehicles. Griffith, the father of narrative film, himself made two biblical epics, *Judith of Bethulia* in 1913 and *Intolerance* in 1916. The continuing viability of the genre became evident in the number of successful remakes of these epics. *Quo Vadis?* was made three times; *Ben Hur* likewise three times; *King of Kings, The Sign of the Cross*, and *The Ten Commandments* each twice.

The biblical spectacular is almost defined as much by style as by content. It is notable for its long takes, boom shots, theatrical sets, and intrusive musical scores. One thinks of the 107-foot crane shot of the Exodus in Cecil B. DeMille's *The Ten Commandments* (1956) or the melodramatic musical pauses of Nicholas Ray's *King of Kings* (1961). As for content, these films tend to focus on the plight of one character of torn allegiance—Moses in the recent *Prince of Egypt*, for example. The crisis is typically conveyed through melodramatic camera gestures, focusing most often on facial expressions in close-up. When the conflict is resolved and the character realigned to a position of orthodoxy, the moment is celebrated in the fashion discussed as "sacramental" in the previous chapter.

The Hollywood epic experienced its greatest success in the 1930s and 1950s, the same decades that saw the rise of musicals, westerns, and horror/sci-fi films. The thirties saw three large successes—*The Sign of the Cross* (1932), *The Crusades* (1935), and *The Last Days of Pompeii* (1935). In the fifties, six of the biggest box-office successes were religious epics—*Samson and Delilah* (1949), *Quo Vadis?* (1951), *David and Bathsheba* (1951), *The Robe* (1953), *The Ten Commandments* (1956), and *Ben Hur* (1959).

The reasons for these outbursts in Hollywood religiosity seem apparent. The country in the thirties experienced a revival of moralism and community conscience as a result of the New Deal after the raucous and destructive twenties. This was the era that produced such morality plays as *I Am a Fugitive from a Chain Gang* (1932), *Angels with Dirty* Faces (1938), *Wild Boys of the Road* (1933), and *The Grapes of Wrath* (1940). Similarly, the fifties, marked heavily by Cold War neurosis and

McCarthyism, produced a similar popular moralism. The religious epic seemed to provide a format compatible with both social milieux, particularly since America's political structure has been built upon the rhetoric of our Christian settlers. The Christian community in the epics of the thirties could function allegorically as the new America that was needed to correct the wild America of the twenties. The Christians in the films of the fifties, simple-hearted and peaceful in the face of Roman oppression, suggested the place of America in a world threatened by communism.

If this seems a bit far-fetched, consider a representative film from each period. In Cecil B. DeMille's *The Sign of the Cross* (1932), Rome is brought to life in images emphasizing its hedonism and sexual debauchery, while the Christians are visualized as particularly poor and chaste. Nero has begun a wholesale persecution of the Christians, whom he blames for the great Roman fire, and his mad rage grows in proportion to the meekness of the suffering believers. In a subplot, a romance develops between a Roman officer, Marcus (Fredric March), and a Christian girl, Mercia (Elissa Landi); despite the vigorous attempts at seduction by Marcus, she refuses to marry an atheist. He, on the other hand, refuses to believe—his hard experiences running counter to belief in a God-ordered universe. Nevertheless, when Mercia is sentenced to die by Nero's hand, Marcus chooses to die with her, and so shares her faith. The resolution is less the triumph of Christianity, given the setup, than it is the triumph of romance, family, strength of character, and personal sacrifice over hedonism and cruelty.

In the much-loved 1959 version of *Ben Hur*, starring Charlton Heston and directed by William Wyler, the focus shifts from the debauchery and madness of Rome to its military force. Two friends, Messala (Stephen Boyd), a Roman, and Judah Ben

Hur, a Jew, become separate from each other through a series of accidents and then further divide due to their ethnic and political allegiances. Ben Hur ends up a galley slave, only to rise again to new social status through the help of a sympathetic rich man. He is given opportunity to avenge himself on the Romans in the famous chariot race in which his primary opponent, as one expects, turns out to be Messala. He would advance further as a Jewish revolutionary if not for the sudden conversion of his mother and sister to Jesus. He sees Jesus Himself at the crucifixion and eventually converts. Like *The Sign of the Cross, Ben Hur* sets Christianity against a very specific context—the threat of Roman domination in the first century, which dovetails nicely with America's plight in the 1950s.

The same sort of contextualization of a Christian story is evident in the greatest of the biblical spectaculars of the 1960s, that being Nicolas Ray's *King of Kings* (1961). This film was released at the start of the Kennedy era and picked up much of the mythos of that period. The Jesus of the Ray film is played by the handsome, blue-eyed Jeffrey Hunter, a heartthrob at the time, prompting the comic trade-name of *King of Kings*, "I Was a Teenage Jesus." His mother Mary, played by the Irish actress Siobhan McKenna, seems to have walked off a Catholic Christmas card. John Fitzgerald Kennedy, of course, was Catholic. And, in fact, this film adds to the story bits of Catholic tradition typically withheld from Protestant Jesus films, like the Veronica cloth (a woman wipes Jesus' face with a cloth on the way to Calvary), the names of the wise men, and the emphasis of Jesus' "sacred heart" of love.

The religious spectacular broke down after a few efforts in the early sixties, perhaps corresponding with the breakdown in American optimism after Vietnam and Watergate. One effort to revive the form illustrates how vacant it had become (whether because of a loss of national fervor or because of a dismissal of the orthodox Christian tradition is rather difficult to determine). This was in a 1985 film called *King David* by the fine Australian director of *Black Robe*, Bruce Beresford. The film, in the spirit of *King of Kings*, starred the pretty-faced Richard Gere in the title role, but unlike the earlier epics it proved to be a dismal box-office failure.

Beresford's *King David* makes plain that a shift had occurred by the mid-eighties in how biblical materials were to be handled in mainstream American film. As weak as the older epics are when examined carefully with Bible in hand, the source Christian texts are still given marginal authority. Cecil B. DeMille could tamper with the details of the book of Exodus to allow for popular tastes in his romantic subplots, but the primary direction of those texts was upheld—Pharaoh would let the people go, and the Ten Commandments would be written in stone by the finger of God. In *King David* many of the scriptural details are presented with a measure of accuracy; yet the direction of the story overall is changed.

The film begins with the scene of Samuel beheading the king of the Amalekites, a rebuke to Saul who was to have done the deed if he had followed the command of God. Saul (Edward Woodward) is cursed by Samuel, who holds before him the gory head of the Amalekite king in a lingering shot that seems designed to tell the viewer that this film will be "realistic." Such sensational moments of graphic violence are pretty much the extent of the film's realism. The emotional center of the story is in a brutal battle sequence that ends with the killing of Saul and Jonathan, a sequence "off-screen" in the actual book of Samuel but on-screen in a vision of David in this film. Ironically, this equation of graphic sensational shots equalling "realism" is one that prior to 1970 had been aligned exclusively with horror films, war films, or pornography.

Beresford's film evokes an aura of social relevancy through a similar reduction. A clear parallel between Saul and David is forced in the film by filling in certain biblical gaps. Saul's fall from favor is played out as a consequence of too much royal luxury and carnality. This will be developed as the source of David's principal troubles too, in his sin with Bathsheba and in his design to build a temple to house the ark of the covenant—here a thing coming from pride, not zeal for the Lord. Playing David so similar to Saul creates a certain kind of audience sympathy in that both men experience the corruptions of power, a subject American audiences have become all too familiar with in the last few decades. Yet, the subtle change cuts the heart out of the biblical account of David's life. David is played throughout as a man unsettled in his relationship with God. From his deathbed he tells his son Solomon to follow the instincts of his heart and then expresses the hope that he might see God's face. The hope is met by a blackened screen and then the film credits. Since both Saul and David had spent the whole film following the instincts of their hearts and it led to little good, this conclusion is hardly triumphant (not that David's end was marked by glorious sanctity if you read the account in Scripture, but certainly his faith at death was better defined than this). What seems to have happened here is that the biblical record was amended to better suit an era drowning in narcissism.

The choice of Gere, who is painfully weak in the lead role, adds to the final effect. It is a long-standing tradition in biblical epics to cast according to physical types rather than historical accuracy or acting prowess—think of Jeffrey Hunter, Charlton Heston, Victor Mature, or Jennifer Jones. The boy who plays the young David has distinctively Jewish features, but a fast-forward

through his adolescent years converts him into the bland mati-
nee idol Gere, whose physical beauty becomes a plot element in
the scene when he dances in a loincloth before the ark, first
attracting the notice of Bathsheba, played by the South African-
born beauty Alice Krige. It might be remembered that Gere's
career developed rapidly after he was displayed nude in Paul
Schrader's *American Gigolo* (1980). When David sees
Bathsheba bathing, there is a link formed between his voyeurism
and hers toward him earlier. The viewer likewise is invited to
desire them both in similar fashion. David gets caught in a sin
of the flesh, but the viewer is made to sympathize through these
links, and so the sin becomes a kind of inevitability. Just as the
narcissism and faithlessness of the popular culture gets projected
onto the biblical story, so does the sexual indulgence.

The shifts in the tradition evident in Beresford's *King David*
help to explain some of the disturbing shifts evident in the next
significant biblical epic in the eighties, Martin Scorsese's *The
Last Temptation of Christ* (1988). Scorsese clearly intended to
create modern relevance for the story of Jesus in *Last
Temptation*, perhaps somewhat in the tradition of the pop musicals of the seventies—*Godspell* (1973) and *Jesus Christ
Superstar* (1973). Yet, he did so not through pop retellings of the
gospel story like those films, but by recreating the older form of
the biblical epic but with a different Jesus.

The film goes further than *King David* in secularizing the
older genre in that the source material isn't even ostensibly the
Bible, for Scorsese follows instead the narrative of Nikos
Kazantzakis's controversial novel *The Last Temptation* (1961).
The story primarily follows Jesus' fictional temptation to leave
the cross and pursue marriage with Mary Magdalene, although
Scorsese also spends a good part of the film developing Jesus'
internal struggle with God's call, as well as his years as a car-

penter. What results is a film version of New Testament apocryphal literature. The justification for the material seemed to be that the New Testament didn't explicitly rule out what Kazantzakis had dreamed up.

I believe that the large public outcry against this Scorsese film in part responded to the alteration brought to the sacred cow of the biblical spectacular. The scenes of public protest around theaters showing the film recall similar scenes whenever Griffith's racially inflammatory *Birth of a Nation* (1915) or Leni Riefenstahl's tribute to Hitler, *Triumph of the Will* (1935), have been publicly shown. The protests were rooted in a deeply felt outrage at the social transgressions of the film—after all, it was just one film, and a rather mediocre one at that. Outside the Biograph Theater in Chicago, where I lived at the time, protesters shouted the Lord's Prayer at ticket-paying customers, irrational behavior regardless of the cause.

What seemed to have happened was that Scorsese's film inadvertently challenged the authority of a weakened church in America, attempting a form of pop evangelism, yet with a gospel story seen by most as a corruption of the Bible. The demythologizing of the biblical spectacular symbolized the destruction of the remaining vestiges of orthodox Christianity in the popular culture. The response of certain evangelicals was particularly telling. The major Christian television network in Chicago urged viewers to boycott the film and showed a counter film, the *Jesus* film produced by Campus Crusade for Christ, with a telephone help line superimposed on the bottom of the screen.

I used the term *pop evangelism* above because *The Last Temptation of Christ* ends on an extremely upbeat note with Jesus triumphantly returning to the cross and with the film celebrating that choice. Also, the film begs to be taken as a serious attempt to rethink the Gospel narratives from an enlightened contemporary point of view. There are actually a couple of moments in the film when Willem Dafoe's portrayal of Jesus seems credible. However, in the main the film fails on all levels to convince and comes across as more of an assault on the film genre than on the Bible. After all, the biblical spectacular had always allowed for certain unorthodoxies—supplemental sub-plots (*Ben Hur*, *King of Kings*), sermonic elaborations of biblical materials, extravagant characterizations (*The Ten Commandments*), and even sentimental, somewhat gnostic por-trayals of Christ (*The Greatest Story Ever Told*). But no other epic had set out to retell and thus improve the story of Jesus.

Before examining *Last Temptation* more closely, it is useful to note that the controversy was foreshadowed three years ear-lier with the release of Jean-Luc Godard's *Hail Mary* in 1984. In this French production a young Swiss virgin girl becomes preg-nant without intercourse. Her cab driver boyfriend suffers through the confusing circumstances with her and then decides to marry her, as in the Gospels but without angelic announce-ments. The child is born and grows, his aloofness troubling Mary and Joseph. Mary develops into an ordinary sensual woman. Godard's intent is, like Scorsese's, to show the spiritual struggles of ordinary people and to provide contemporary rele-vance to the Gospel narrative. Many of Godard's compositions in the film linger like still-life paintings and evoke an aura of mystery around the characters and events. Whenever Mary's body is displayed naked, the poses are graceful and painterly. A subplot in the film has a college professor contemplating whether the body has a soul or the soul a body, Godard obvi-ously suggesting the latter, that the universe is a result of spiri-tuality taking on materiality.

Hail Mary never achieved the level of controversy in the States that *Last Temptation* did, but it was condemned as blasphemous by Pope John Paul II and Cardinal O'Connor and blocked from release on American cable networks. Its difference from *Last Temptation* was twofold; it was a foreign film, and a French one at that, and it was more allegory than biblical epic. Yet, it was something of a warning shot of what was to come.

Last Temptation has all of the elements of the older biblical epics—location sets, reverential compositions, musical cues to divine actions, and, of course, the main characters. It also builds toward the grand "sacramental moment" I have described, this being the final shot when the camera freezes on the jubilant face of Jesus, back from his temptation to leave the cross and marry. The screen flashes brilliant colors after this image, and bells ring in the background while the credits roll.

Where the film diverges from the epic pattern is in the continuous attempts to draw the viewers into full sympathy with Jesus as man, not God-man, something that Christians tend not to do in any artistic medium. Frequent close-ups of Willem Dafoe emphasize Jesus' struggles to be understood and to secure His call from God. Also, His temptations are of a highly speculative nature—first as He watches Mary Magdalene servicing customers in a brothel, then as He is forced to aid in a Roman crucifixion, and later as He must plead for Judas' support. Perhaps if the film had one such detail, it might have come across as less of an intentional attempt to incite, but it layers scene upon scene of this sort, without allowing much respite for viewers who might like to think things over.

One other curious twist in the film is the omission of any genuine triumphs, unless one counts the return of Jesus to the cross. When Jesus raises Lazarus from the dead, the moment is undercut by the suggestion of the physical repugnance of the three-day corrupted man; Lazarus is then later murdered. The sick who

Willem Dafoe as Jesus blesses the children in Martin
Scorsese's *The Last Temptation of Christ* (1988).

ask for Jesus' help are portrayed as a wailing and horrible mass,
inspiring no genuine sympathy. Even Judas' betrayal and Jesus'
response at the Last Supper get reversed as the Jesus of this film
actually asks Judas to betray Him since He will not be the leader
against Rome that Judas wants.

In the last temptation, an angelic girl comes to Jesus as He
hangs on the cross and leads Him down from it, suggesting He
has done enough. She dresses His wounds and encourages Him
to go off and become a husband and father, which He does. He
first marries Mary Magdalene, and then after her death he marries Mary of Bethany (as well as Martha, the narrative suggests).
His life is simple and fulfilled as He works quietly and raises children and grows old. Only in the film's concluding scene is conflict reintroduced.

In this scene Jesus is lying on his deathbed, tended by the
angelic girl who praises Him for the choices He has made.
Suddenly Jesus' former disciples appear at His door to warn
Him that the girl is a temptress and that the world still needs sav-

ing. Outside the door, the sky looks overtaken by storm, a surrealistic red darkness. The girl then transforms into Satan, paradoxically in a pillar of fire, who begins to mock. At this, Jesus cries out and crawls from the bed and back to the cross. The journey is dreamlike and eerie, culminating in the triumphal return mentioned above.

Implausible and tasteless as this all is, Scorsese actually softened the Kazantzakis novel, which has passages that seem borrowed from some Harlequin romance: "Jesus seized her, threw back her head and kissed her on the mouth. They both turned deathly pale. Their knees gave way. Unable to go further, they lay down under a flowering lemon-tree and began to roll on the ground. . . . Purring, Mary Magdalene hugged the man, kept his body glued to hers."

Once all the rhetoric gets scratched away from *The Last Temptation of Christ*, not much of substance is left. It is a painfully confused work that would be downright laughable if not for its offensiveness. It follows thematically the pattern of most popular films of the seventies and eighties. It first presents a character torn by mixed allegiance in search of an integrated and guilt-free identity. Second, it defines the inner conflict as principally sexual. Third, it builds from one sensational image to another in the manner of soft-core pornography—the brothel scene, the first crucifixion, the desert temptations, the meeting with John, etc.

What Scorsese has done is taken a dead genre, the biblical spectacular, and tried to realign it for new effect. He fails, but the attempt, whether intentional or not, reveals much about social and moral changes in America in the late eighties. It is significant that the next attempt to do a biblical epic was an animated film, *The Prince of Egypt* in 1998. Many evangelicals celebrated this effort, which in itself has some merit. In the context of the tradition of biblical epics in American film, however, the event of an animated biblical epic aimed primarily at children hardly seems to be a cultural breakthrough.

When genres die in film, they usually mutate into some other form. Westerns, for example, got transferred to the emerging sci-fi genre after the success of *Star Wars*. The biblical spectacular melted into epic fantasy films like *Excalibur* (1981), *Ladyhawke* (1985), The *Princess Bride* (1987), and *Willow* (1988). Echoes of it can also be heard in films of interplanetary commerce like *Close Encounters of the Third Kind* (1977), *E.T.* (1982), *The Terminator* (1984), and *Cocoon* (1985).

There have been several films in more recent years that have gotten past the reverential treatment of Christian subjects that was the legacy of the old spectaculars, and perhaps this is a good result of their demise. Films like *Chariots of Fire* (1981), *Tender Mercies* (1982), *The Trip to Bountiful* (1985), and, most recently, *The Apostle* (1998) have taken more honest looks at the lives of Christian people and thus have perhaps been more influential than the old stylized productions. The danger of the old spectaculars was that a person might see one and conclude he has learned about the Bible. Films like *The Apostle*, which tell the tale of real Christians, albeit flawed ones, do not purport to tell Bible stories and so might lead people to the Book itself.

The fact to remember in this short history is that the cultural Christianity that had produced the great biblical epics was always just that, a cultural Christianity, often using the biblical stories to promote other important political and ideological issues. Its rapid death after the turbulent sixties and seventies suggests more about American culture than American Christianity. Although the aftermath has shaken the church, evidenced by the shocked outrage generated by *Last Temptation*, the results might be that Christians see better their place in this culture, which is to be salt and light in a depraved and despairing world.

> *We have not received the spirit of the world but the Spirit who is from God, that we may understand what God has freely given us.*
>
> —*1 Corinthians 2:12*, NIV

NOTES FOR CHAPTER 7

1. This argument is played out in greater detail in Peter Fraser, *Images of the Passion: The Sacramental Mode in Film* (New York: Praeger, 1998), 163-182.

CHAPTER EIGHT

A REVIEWER'S GUIDE
BY VERNON EDWIN NEAL

⑤

In South Africa workers mine for diamonds; in Alaska they drill for oil. People on beaches wave metal detectors over the sand in the hope of finding valuable items left behind by bathers. Millions play the lottery, enter sweepstakes, and play at casinos hoping to hit it rich.

People work long and hard to find treasures. For the film lover and critic it is no different; we often wade through many horrible films to find quality features. It is often hard to know in advance whether a film will be good or bad, since even the worst productions are packaged as great masterpieces. First come the elaborate trailers you see at the theater months in advance of the release. Then follow the television ads that reinforce the trailers, followed by the procession of the film stars who begin to make the rounds of the network talk shows and appear on the covers of the grocery store magazines. It is all part of the pop cultural flow, the seamless network of commercial promotion based upon the notion that all Americans will buy product if the packaging is attractive.

The average American watches television four to five hours per day, which, given a seventy-year average lifespan, translates into something like eleven continuous years of twenty-four hour days given wholly to the electric voice of pop culture. Even the careful Christian trying to resist the homogenizing voice of pop falls at times to its allurements. Like it or not, when that hot new film hits the theaters, we can't wait to see it, if only to keep in touch. We just must go see, we say, *The Blair Witch Project* or whatever.

Opening day arrives, and we rush to the local theater, pay our $6.75 or more admission price, and go in. The houselights go down, and after commercials and more trailers, the movie starts and we are captive to the screen for the next 90 to 120 minutes or even longer; nothing else matters.

In twenty-five years of reviewing, I have gone through this experience hundreds of times. I have received countless invitations to advance screenings for movies that, you would think from the press kits, are each to be the next *Citizen Kane*.

These press kits are a subject all to themselves. The press kit for *Godzilla*, for example, has on a glossy cover the words "Size Does Matter." The word "Godzilla" is in raised black capital letters. When you open the kit, through the wonders of modern technology, you actually hear Godzilla roar. Now, who can resist that?

Yet, to do my job effectively, I have to resist the hype and make sensible choices about the films I will see and review. Then I have to think carefully about whether I want to recommend a film or not. Many people will give attention to what I say, and I take this as a serious responsibility. In order to recommend a film to my reading public I have to ask: 1) How was the film overall? 2) Did the cast work well together to make audiences believe their characters? 3) Did technical matters like photography, sets, special effects, and so on enhance or detract from the overall success of the film? 4) Was the violence, sexuality, and language too graphic or degrading for audiences? I think through the answer to these questions and make my decision.

Even when people disagree with my positions, I know I can create interesting conversation, and that in itself is highly useful. I want to make people think along with me and evaluate wisely, and thus not fall prey themselves to the advertising blitz.

Often I share my commentary with several close friends around the country: Olin and Carol Ridling, Max and Christine Alvarez, Miss Jean Nelson, and Mr. Brian Niemiec. Because I see many films in advance, I let them know if they should rush out to see a new release or wait for the video. When they see the film, we talk. It is a good system of checks and balances.

Today people have a remarkable number of choices of films to see through theaters, video, cable, or satellite dish. Long gone are the days when people were limited to the two films playing at the neighborhood theater.

When looking at ads for new films on television or in the newspapers, it is good to remember that the particular studio releasing the film is *selling* that film. It is also good to realize that positive reviews of films can be manufactured in a variety of ways. Finding people you can trust to make discerning recommendations consistently is a great blessing.

We compiled the lists of films that follow to represent features on a range of topics. From our points of view, they are all worth watching for the questions they raise and for their artistic merits, not necessarily for their content. If a person is interested in exploring film as art, particularly from a Christian point of view, here is a place to start, a guide.

The list is organized by categories that we thought had the most contemporary relevance. We list at least ten films in each category and then offer some basic information to get viewers started. If we accomplish nothing else, we might at least make your weekly visits to Blockbuster or the library shorter. But, of course, we hope we will accomplish more than that.

CHRISTIANITY AND FILM

Of all the films made in this past century that address Christianity head-on with great artistry and integrity, these may be the best.

Open City, 1945, directed by Roberto Rossellini and starring Aldo Fabrizi, Anna Magnani, Marcello Pagliero, and Harry Feist. A gritty account of Italian resistance to fascism and the courage of those martyred for the cause.

Diary of a Country Priest, 1950, directed by Robert Bresson and starring Claude Laydu, Nicole Ladmiral, Jean Riveyre, and Nicole Maurey. A classic French film about a young priest, gravely ill, who ministers to an indifferent rural parish.

On the Waterfront, 1954, directed by Elia Kazan and star-

Marlon Brando as Terry Malloy seeking penance in Elia Kazan's *On the Waterfront* (1954).

ring Marlon Brando, Karl Malden, Eva Marie Saint, Rod Steiger, and Lee J. Cobb. One of America's greatest films, this story of a down-and-out dockworker who must turn against his peers to redeem himself and break up a corrupt union has some of the most memorable dramatic scenes ever filmed.

Ordet, 1955, directed by Carl Dreyer and starring Henrik Malberg, Emil Hass Christensen, and Preben Lerdorff Rye. A stunning drama about conflict between two Lutheran families and, ultimately, between dead orthodoxy and true faith.

Andrei Rublev, 1966, directed by Andrei Tarkovsky and starring Anatoli Solonitzine, Ivan Lapikov, Nikolai Grinko, and Nikolai Sergueiev. Sweeping historical drama of Russia's great fifteenth-century icon painter and the spiritual conflicts he faced in those brutal times.

The Gospel According to St. Matthew, 1966, directed by Pier Paolo Pasolini and starring Enrique Irazoqui, Margherita Caruso, Susanna Pasolini, Marcello Morante, and Mario Socrate. There is this film on the life of Jesus and then all the other ones. An unconventional depiction of Christ's life that follows Matthew's Gospel literally and maintains authenticity throughout. A landmark.

The Mission, 1986, directed by Roland Joffe and starring Robert DeNiro, Jeremy Irons, Liam Neeson. Interesting character study of two Jesuit priests who combat the political and religious corruption of eighteenth-century Brazil in far different ways. Haunting imagery and provocative content make this film remarkable.

Babette's Feast, 1987, directed by Gabriel Axel and starring Stephane Audran, Birgitte Federspiel, Bodil Kjer, Jean-Philippe LaFont, Jarl Kulle, and Bibi Andersson. Exquisite tale of two daughters of a strict pietist sectarian who find redemption in old age through a Parisian refugee cook. More than an allegory about art and life, this film speaks eloquently about life itself.

Black Robe, 1991, directed by Bruce Beresford and starring Lothaire Bluteau, August Schellenberg, Aden Young, and Sandrine Holt. A brilliant and honest film based on the diary of martyred French Jesuit Noel Chabanel who brought the Gospel to Indians in seventeenth-century Quebec.

The Apostle, 1998, directed by Robert Duvall and starring Robert Duvall and Farrah Fawcett. Interesting examination of a showy Pentecostal preacher who has fatal human flaws, yet continues to advance the Gospel.

RELIGION IN FILM

These films look at religion defined more broadly. The list provides a mixed bag in terms of content and quality, yet all have interest.

Going My Way, 1944, directed by Leo McCarey and starring Bing Crosby, Barry Fitzgerald, and Frank McHugh. A progressive young priest is assigned to get a poor parish out of debt, but the ranking older priest is set in his ways.

Quo Vadis?, 1951, directed by Mervyn LeRoy and starring Robert Taylor, Deborah Kerr, and Peter Ustinov. This film about persecution of Christians by the Emperor Nero has a continuing appeal, unlike many other films of the period.

The Nun's Story, 1959, directed by Fred Zinnemann and starring Audrey Hepburn, Peter Finch, Edith Evans, and Dean Jagger. A young nun struggles with difficult experiences in the Congo and Belgium during World War II.

Elmer Gantry, 1960, directed by Richard Brooks and starring Burt Lancaster, Shirley Jones, Jean Simmons, and Patti Page. A small-town evangelist in the early 1920s smooth-talks himself into the big time until scandal breaks around him.

Inherit the Wind, 1960, directed by Stanley Kramer and starring Spencer Tracy, Fredric March, and Gene Kelly. The Scopes

"Monkey Trial" of 1925 is the basis of this film as a small town ruled by religion wants to make sure evolution isn't taught in their schools.

A Man for All Seasons, 1968, directed by Fred Zinnemann and starring Paul Scofield, Robert Shaw, and Orson Welles. This multiple Oscar-winning film deals with the battle between Sir Thomas More and King Henry VIII who wants to divorce his wife Catherine of Aragon to marry mistress Anne Boleyn and produce an heir.

In This House of Brede, 1975, directed by George Schaefer and starring Diana Rigg, Jodi Bowker, and Pamela Brown. A successful London businesswoman gives up her worldly life to become a cloistered Benedictine nun.

The Chosen, 1981, directed by Jeremy Paul Kagan and starring Robby Benson, Barry Miller, Maximilian Schell, and Rod Steiger. Two Brooklyn teenagers form a friendship in 1940. One has a father who is a Hassidic rabbi, while the other's father is a Zionist professor. From the great Chaim Potok novel.

The Last Temptation of Christ, 1988, directed by Martin Scorsese and starring Willem Dafoe, Harvey Keitel, Barbara Hershey, and David Bowie. Controversial, albeit mediocre, film that asks how Christ might have had to deal with human desires and questions of His own divinity.

Life Is Beautiful, 1998, directed by Roberto Benigni and starring Roberto Benigni, Nicolette Braschi, Giorgio Cantarini, and Giustino Durano. Not a religious film on the surface, but one so moving and life-affirming and with such a resonant conclusion that it can only belong in this category. This Chaplinesque story of one man's attempts to preserve beauty in the most horrible circumstances may well prove to be one of the finest films ever made.

LOVE AND ROMANCE

These films look at the wonderful ways that romance draws ordinary people into extraordinary relationships.

The Guardsman, 1931, directed by Sidney Franklin and starring Alfred Lunt, Lynn Fontanne, Roland Young, and ZaSu Pitts. This superb comedy showcased great, little-known talents. A jealous husband tests his wife's love by donning a disguise and trying to seduce her, but she knows it's him.

A Farewell to Arms, 1932, directed by Frank Borzage and starring Helen Hayes, Gary Cooper, Adolphe Menjou, and Jack LaRue. In Italy during World War I an American ambulance driver and an English nurse begin a tragic love affair. The ending differs from that in the Hemingway novel.

Casablanca, 1942, directed by Michael Curtiz and starring Humphrey Bogart, Ingrid Bergman, Paul Henreid, Dooley Wilson, and Claude Rains. Classic World War II love story set

A memorable pairing of Humphrey Bogart and Sydney Greenstreet in Michael Curtiz's *Casablanca* (1942).

in Casablanca where everyone comes to Rick's Cafe. It's going well until an old flame of Rick's shows up one night with her husband.

Woman of the Year, 1942, directed by George Stevens and starring Spencer Tracy, Katharine Hepburn, and Fay Bainter. A smart female political columnist and a gruff but charming sports writer working on the same paper meet, fall in love, and marry. The fun is in what follows.

Brief Encounter, 1946, directed by David Lean and starring Celia Johnson, Trevor Howard, and Stanley Holloway. One of the most poignant and lyrical films ever made. Two middle-aged, married people happen into a bittersweet romance. Bring Kleenex.

The African Queen, 1951, directed by John Huston and starring Humphrey Bogart, Katharine Hepburn, and Robert Morley. American classic of a strict missionary and a hard-drinking expatriate who must travel together downriver in Africa. They take on the Germans for good measure.

Sabrina, 1954, directed by Billy Wilder and starring Humphrey Bogart, Audrey Hepburn, William Holden, John Williams, and Martha Hyer. Two rich brothers, one a playboy and the other a hard-working businessman, fall in love with their chauffeur's spirited daughter, played by Audrey Hepburn.

A Room with a View, 1986, directed by James Ivory and starring Helena Bonham Carter, Julian Sands, Denholm Elliott, Maggie Smith, and Judi Dench. A feisty English idealist rejects a dashing fellow for a supercilious one, then fights her passion.

Much Ado About Nothing, 1993, directed by Kenneth Branagh and starring Kenneth Branagh, Emma Thompson, Denzel Washington, and Kate Beckinsale. A truly great version of the Shakespeare play about two sets of lovers "battling." Branagh and Thompson have remarkable chemistry on screen.

Sleepless in Seattle, 1993, directed by Nora Ephron and starring Tom Hanks, Meg Ryan, Bill Pullman, and Rita Wilson. A widower shares on a national radio talk show about his deceased wife, and a recently engaged woman, touched by what he said, finds him.

FILMS ABOUT THE FAMILY AND FOR THE FAMILY

Not all sweetness and light, these films show families dealing with problems realistically and surviving.

The Biscuit Eater, 1940, directed by Stuart Heisler and starring Billy Lee, Cordell Hickman, Helene Millard, and Richard Lane. This bittersweet little film follows two boys, one black and one white, who work to turn an unwanted puppy into a champion bird dog.

The Grapes of Wrath, 1940, directed by John Ford and starring Henry Fonda, Jane Darwell, and John Carradine. A brilliant film based on the Steinbeck novel about an Oklahoma family leaving the dust bowl in search of a better life in California.

Our Town, 1940, directed by Sam Wood and starring Martha Scott, William Holden, and Thomas Mitchell. The simple life of New England small-towners in 1900s is the theme of this classic Thornton Wilder play.

How Green Was My Valley, 1941, directed by John Ford and starring Walter Pidgeon, Maureen O'Hara, and Roddy McDowall. Saga of a Welsh mining family struggling for survival in the most depressing of circumstances.

The Yearling, 1946, directed by Clarence Brown and starring Gregory Peck, Jane Wyman, and Claude Jarman, Jr. In post-Civil War Florida, a young boy's love for a yearling fawn teaches his family some powerful life lessons.

Cheaper by the Dozen, 1950, directed by Walter Lang and starring Clifton Webb, Myrna Loy, and Jeanne Crain. A turn-of-the-century efficiency expert tries his ideas on his wife and twelve children with unusual and sometimes comic results.

Old Yeller, 1957, directed by Robert Stevenson and starring Dorothy McGuire, Fess Parker, Tommy Kirk, Kevin Corcoran, and Chuck Connors. Two young brothers caring for the family farm while their father is away adopt a stray dog, but a tragedy occurs that will change everyone's life.

The Swiss Family Robinson, 1960, directed by Ken Annakin and starring John Mills, Dorothy McGuire, and James MacArthur. A family escaping from Napoleonic war is shipwrecked on a beautiful abandoned island near New Guinea. Life goes well until pirates come calling.

The Parent Trap, 1961, directed by David Swift and starring Hayley Mills, Maureen O'Hara, and Brian Keith. Twin sisters meet for the first time at summer camp and decide to get their divorced parents back together. The recent remake can't top the charm of Hayley Mills.

The Sound of Music, 1965, directed by Robert Wise and starring Julie Andrews, Christopher Plummer, Eleanor Parker, Angela Cartwright, and Richard Haydn. This true story about the singing Von Trapp family of Austria and their daring escape from the Nazis is still heartwarming and moving with beautiful scenery, great music, and fine acting.

The One and Only, Genuine Original Family Band, 1968, directed by Michael O'Herlihy and starring Walter Brennan, Kurt Russell, and Goldie Hawn. The presidential election between Benjamin Harrison and Grover Cleveland divides a once harmonious and talented group of family musicians, producing interesting situations.

A Christmas Story, 1983, directed by Bob (Benjamin) Clark and starring Peter Billingsley, Darren McGavin, and Melinda

Dillon. A modern comedy classic about a little boy who wants a BB gun for Christmas.

To Sleep with Anger, 1990, directed by Charles Burnett and starring Danny Glover, Mary Alice, Paul Butler, and Vonetta McGee. A middle-class black family in Los Angeles is troubled when a sly charmer and family friend shows up at the door.

A River Runs Through It, 1992, directed by Robert Redford and starring Tom Skerritt, Craig Scheffer, Brad Pitt, and Brenda Blethyn. A poignant and beautiful film about two brothers whose lives drift in different directions. Easily one of the best films of the nineties with gorgeous cinematography and brilliant performances all around to accompany a wonderfully literate script.

Soul Food, 1997, directed by George J. R. Tillman and starring Vanessa Williams, Vivica A. Fox, Nia Long, Emma P. Hall, and Mekki Phifer. A black family must learn to cope without the stabilizing presence of a beloved mother. Told powerfully through the eyes of her grandson.

FILMS FOR YOUNGER CHILDREN

For children between five and ten, film can teach as well as entertain. Here are some of the better films that do both.

The Little Colonel, 1935, directed by David Butler and starring Shirley Temple, Lionel Barrymore, Evelyn Venable, and Bill "Bojangles" Robinson. The highlight of the film is Shirley dancing with the great Bill Robinson, but other cast members elevate this story of reconciliation as well.

The 5,000 Fingers of Dr. T, 1953, directed by Roy Rowland and starring Peter Lind Hayes, Mary Healy, Tommy Rettig, and Hans Conried. A boy runs away from piano lessons into an adventure in this memorable only screenplay written by the great Theodore "Dr. Seuss" Geisel.

Mary Poppins, 1964, directed by Robert Stevenson and starring Julie Andrews, Dick Van Dyke, David Tomlinson, Glynis Johns, and Ed Wynn. A fairy-tale nanny gives a proper English banker a chance to get close once more to his family.

Chitty Chitty Bang Bang, 1968, directed by Ken Hughes and starring Dick Van Dyke, Sally Ann Howes, and Lionel Jeffries. An oddball inventor repairs an old car and takes his two children on an adventure they will never forget.

The Black Stallion, 1979, directed by Carroll Ballard and starring Kelly Reno, Mickey Rooney, Teri Garr, and Clarence Muse. A gorgeously filmed story of trust between a young boy and an Arabian stallion who survive a shipwreck together.

The NeverEnding Story, 1984, directed by Wolfgang Petersen and starring Barret Oliver, Noah Hathaway, Gerald MacRaney, and Moses Gunn. This remarkable Michael Ende story of a boy who enters a book to save a warrior's fantasy world promotes the wonders of reading.

Beauty and the Beast, 1991, directed by Kirk Wise and Gary Trousdale. One of the several fine film versions of the classic fairy tale about looks and realities, this one took Disney animation to an entirely new level. Oscar-winning score by Alan Menken is just one of the perks.

The Lion King, 1994, directed by Rob Minkoff and Roger Allers. One of the best recent Disney efforts, this excellent animated film tells the story of a young lion cub who becomes an outcast because of a wicked uncle, only to win back respect. The story recalls the earlier Disney classic *Bambi*.

Toy Story, 1995, directed by John Lasseter. This first great computer-animated feature deals winningly with toys who have a life of their own. Despite the technology, this is a simple tale about friends helping one another, creating characters who will have a permanent place in American culture.

The Iron Giant, 1999, directed by Brad Bird. An exceptional animated feature by Warner Brothers that deals with a young boy who finds and defends a giant robot, leading to a lesson about toleration and peace. The story was originally written in 1968 by English poet laureate Ted Hughes.

DREAMING BIG DREAMS

These inspirational or instructive films show individuals trying to reach goals beyond the ordinary, and so playing out a part of the American dream or its equivalent.

Citizen Kane, 1941, directed by Orson Welles and starring Orson Welles, Joseph Cotton, and Agnes Moorehead. This great American film traces the rise of a media tycoon, based on the life of William Randolph Hearst.

How to Succeed in Business Without Really Trying, 1967, directed by David Swift and starring Robert Morse, Michele Lee, and Rudy Vallee. A New York City window washer reads a self-help book and rises in corporate America with little real talent. A great musical from a winning Broadway production.

Rocky, 1976, directed by John G. Avidsen and starring Sylvester Stallone, Talia Shire, and Burgess Meredith. Popular sleeper about a Philadelphia club boxer given the chance to fight for the heavyweight championship of the world.

The Competition, 1980, directed by Joel Oliansky and starring Richard Dreyfuss, Amy Irving, and Lee Remick. Two gifted pianists meet and fall in love at a competition in which they must play against each other.

Chariots of Fire, 1981, directed by Hugh Hudson and starring Ben Cross, Ian Charleson, and Ian Holm. In the 1924 Olympics two runners compete for England—one for Jewish pride, the other to bring honor to Jesus. This powerful drama won the Academy Award in 1981 to the delight of many Christians.

Flashdance, 1983, directed by Adrian Lyne and starring Jennifer Beals, Michael Nouri, and Cynthia Rhodes. A woman welds by day and dances at clubs at night, dreaming about one day auditioning for a prestigious ballet school.

Stand and Deliver, 1987, directed by Ramon Menendez and starring Edward James Olmos, Lou Diamond Phillips, Rosana de Soto, and Andy Garcia. Inspiring true story of a tough math teacher who inspires East L.A. barrio students to pass an Advanced Placement (AP) test.

City of Joy, 1992, directed by Roland Joffe and starring Patrick Swayze, Pauline Collins, and Om Puri. A disenchanted American heart surgeon loses a patient in New York City and goes to India to forget, only to be changed more than he imagined.

Far and Away, 1992, directed by Ron Howard and starring Tom Cruise, Nicole Kidman, and Colm Meaney. A headstrong young Irishman and his equally spirited girlfriend leave Ireland to settle in America in the 1890s.

October Sky, 1998, directed by Joe Johnson and starring Jake Gyllenhaal, Chris Cooper, William Lee Scott, Chad Lindbergh, and Laura Dern. Based on NASA designer Homer Hickman's autobiography *Rocket Boys*, this moving film tells how four boys overcome the dreariness of their mining community in the 1950s to follow a dream and create a miniature rocket.

DYSFUNCTIONAL FAMILY FILMS

These are films that in a comedic or serious vein look at the family that you don't want to have.

You Can't Take It with You, 1938, directed by Frank Capra

and starring James Stewart, Jean Arthur, and Lionel Barrymore. In New York City a levelheaded young woman from an eccentric family falls in love with a boy from a rich family, leading to comic conflicts.

Arsenic and Old Lace, 1944, directed by Frank Capra and starring Cary Grant, Josephine Hull, Jean Adair, and Jack Carson. Two elderly spinsters advertise rooms for rent for lonely gentlemen, only to spike their elderberry wine with arsenic, in this classic black comedy.

Mildred Pierce, 1945, directed by Michael Curtiz and starring Joan Crawford, Jack Carson, Zachary Scott, and Ann Blyth. A hard-working divorcée tries to make life better for herself and her two daughters, who make the task difficult.

Night of the Hunter, 1955, directed by Charles Laughton and starring Robert Mitchum, Shelley Winters, Lillian Gish, and Peter Graves. A haunting film with Mitchum as a psychotic preacher menacing his own children.

Robert Mitchum plays a murderous preacher of love and hate in Charles Laughton's haunting *Night of the Hunter* (1955).

Cat on a Hot Tin Roof, 1958, directed by Richard Brooks and starring Paul Newman, Burl Ives, Elizabeth Taylor, and Jack Carson. Big Daddy, head of a patriarchal southern family, is dying, and various family members fight for the goods and love.

What Ever Happened to Baby Jane?, 1962, directed by Robert Aldrich and starring Bette Davis, Joan Crawford, and Victor Buono. Two former child stars who are sisters live together in a decrepit mansion and feed on one another. A cruel but fascinating film with great performances.

Carbon Copy, 1981, directed by Michael A. Schultz and starring George Segal, Susan St. James, and Denzel Washington. A prosperous businessman's life gets a shock when his seventeen-year-old illegitimate son comes to visit, opening a door on hidden racism, deceit, and misunderstanding.

Hamlet, 1990, directed by Franco Zeffirelli and starring Mel Gibson, Glenn Close, Alan Bates, and Paul Scofield. This heavy-handed Freudian interpretation of a great Shakespeare play makes for interesting discussion afterward. Surprisingly good performance by Gibson as the Danish prince.

What's Eating Gilbert Grape, 1993, directed by Lasse Hallstrom and starring Johnny Depp, Leonardo DiCaprio, Mary Steenburgen, and Juliette Lewis. The Grape family lives in a small Iowa town, but nothing else is normal as Mother weighs over 500 pounds, and there are two arguing sisters and a seventeen-year-old retarded brother you can't leave alone.

DRINK, DRUGS, AND OTHER VICES

These films explore the terrible effects of addictive behavior on ordinary people.

Greed, 1924, directed by Erich von Stroheim and starring Dale Fuller, ZaSu Pitts, and Jean Hersholt. A greedy wife's

Ray Milland contemplates the disintegration of his life to alcohol in Billy Wilder's *The Lost Weekend* (1945).

obsession with money forces her husband to kill to satisfy her lust, but a terrible price will have to be paid.

Double Indemnity, 1944, directed by Billy Wilder and starring Fred MacMurray, Barbara Stanwyck, and Edward G. Robinson. A poisonous woman "charms" a gullible insurance agent into a plot to kill her husband for his insurance money in this classic *film noir*.

The Lost Weekend, 1945, directed by Billy Wilder and starring Ray Milland, Jane Wyman, and Howard de Silva. Milland won an Oscar for his role as a talented alcoholic writer left alone over the weekend.

The Treasure of the Sierra Madre, 1948, directed by John Huston and starring Humphrey Bogart, Walter Huston, and Tim Holt. Prospectors in Mexico fall prey to greed and betrayal once they get their hands on the yellow metal.

The Hustler, 1961, directed by Robert Rossen and starring Paul Newman, Jackie Gleason, and George C. Scott. The world of professional pool is grimly portrayed as a talented rookie tries to make his mark.

The Days of Wine and Roses, 1962, directed by Blake Edwards and starring Jack Lemmon, Lee Remick, and Jack Klugman. A social-drinking ad man drags his new wife into the world of alcoholism, threatening his home, job, and marriage.

House of Games, 1987, directed by David Mamet and starring Joe Mantegna, Lindsay Crouse, and Mike Nussbaum. A rigidly conventional psychiatrist investigates the secret world of con artists only to find herself drawn in deeper than she imagined.

Clean and Sober, 1988, directed by Glenn Gordon Caron and starring Michael Keaton, Kathy Baker, Morgan Freeman, and M. Emmet Walsh. A drug addict in denial goes to a rehabilitation clinic to get his life together. Keaton drew from personal experience in this fine performance.

The Grifters, 1990, directed by Stephen Frears and starring Anjelica Huston, John Cusack, and Annette Bening. Con artists stay on top by using every slick trick they know to get cash, power, and another day, even against each other.

TALES FROM THE UNDERWORLD

Hollywood has a special knack for producing good films about extremely bad people as evidenced by these titles.

Little Caesar, 1930, directed by Mervyn LeRoy and starring Edward G. Robinson, Glenda Farrell, and Douglas Fairbanks, Jr. A tough hood becomes an even tougher gang leader who rises quickly only to fall quickly.

Scarface, 1931, directed by Howard Hawks and starring Paul Muni and Boris Karloff. The title character is a Chicago gangster in the 1930s whose ruthless rise to the top wins him few friends but many rivals.

Pat O'Brien tries to steer Jimmy Cagney down a better path in Michael Curtiz's *Angels with Dirty Faces* (1938).

Angels with Dirty Faces, 1938, directed by Michael Curtiz and starring James Cagney, Pat O'Brien, and Humphrey Bogart. Two tough young hoods growing up in New York City's east side go different routes, one becoming a priest, the other a criminal. Will the other neighborhood toughs follow the priest or the criminal?

Key Largo, 1948, directed by John Huston and starring Humphrey Bogart, Lauren Bacall, and Edward G. Robinson. A hurricane traps several hoods in a Key West hotel; but the storm inside is equally fierce.

White Heat, 1949, directed by Raoul Walsh and starring James Cagney, Virginia Mayo, and Edmund O'Brien. An emotionally unstable criminal is ruthless in his crimes but tender to his mother.

The Godfather, 1972, *The Godfather, Part 2*, 1974, and *The Godfather, Part 3*, 1990, directed by Francis Ford Coppola and starring Marlon Brando, Al Pacino, Diane Keaton, Talia Shire,

and Robert Duvall. The three films together provide an interesting look at a fictional Mafia family, the Corleones, through
several generations both in Sicily and in America.

Once Upon a Time in America, 1984, directed by Sergio
Leone and starring Robert DeNiro, James Woods, Elizabeth
McGovern, and Tuesday Weld. Five young men living in
Brooklyn in the 1920s grow up to be powerful mobsters. The
film is told through flashbacks as one of the men looks back at
his fifty years of crime.

Things Change, 1988, directed by David Mamet and starring
Joe Mantegna, Don Ameche. and Mike Nussbaum. A minor
hood is sent to bring in an old Italian shoeshine man the mob
needs for a fall guy, but instead takes him to Las Vegas in this
clever black comedy.

The Krays, 1990, directed by Peter Medak and starring Gary
Kemp, Martin Kemp, and Billie Whitelaw. The Krays were two
brothers ruling London's East End in the 1960s who showed no
mercy to anyone getting in their way, but always showed respect
to their strong-willed mother.

Bugsy, 1991, directed by Barry Levinson and starring Warren
Beatty, Annette Bening, and Joe Mantegna. Benjamin "Bugsy"
Siegel was a 1940s gangster who loved Las Vegas's bright lights,
putting him in conflict with the mob.

Donnie Brasco, 1996, directed by Mike Newell and starring
Johnny Depp, Al Pacino, and Bruno Kirby. To get more information on the mob, an FBI agent goes undercover and gets quite close.

PREJUDICE IN THE MOVIES

The American Heritage Dictionary defines prejudice as "the
irrational suspicion or hatred of a particular group, race, or religion." Since film is so popular a medium, how race relations are
depicted in film has always revealed much about our society.

The Birth of a Nation, 1916, directed by D. W. Griffith and starring Lillian Gish, Mae Marsh, Wallace Reid, and Donald Crisp. This disturbing epic, telling the story of the Civil War from a southern point of view, ends with the triumphant ride of the KKK. Rarely shown in public for good reasons.

Dumbo, 1941, directed by Ben Sharpsteen with the voice talents of Sterling Holloway, Verma Felton, and Herman Bing. This Walt Disney animated feature dealing with a baby elephant born in a circus plays as a morality tale about "difference." Too good to be just for kids.

The Ox-Bow Incident, 1943, directed by William Wellman and starring Henry Fonda, Harry Morgan, and Anthony Quinn. Mob justice rules as three innocent cattle buyers are threatened with lynching for the murder of a well-liked rancher, based on circumstantial evidence.

Bad Day at Black Rock, 1954, directed by John Sturges and

Spencer Tracy sits in judgment of Robert Ryan and the whole town of Black Rock in John Sturges's remarkable *Bad Day at Black Rock* (1954).

starring Spencer Tracy, Robert Ryan, Anne Francis, and Ernest Borgnine. After World War II, a one-armed veteran goes to a small western town to repay a debt, only to uncover a terrible secret that the whole town is covering up.

To Kill a Mockingbird, 1962, directed by Robert Mulligan and starring Gregory Peck, Brock Peters, and Robert Duvall. A white southern lawyer defends a black man accused of rape. The story is seen from the point of view of the lawyer's children. Brilliant film with memorable performances.

Guess Who's Coming to Dinner, 1967, directed by Stanley Kramer and starring Katharine Hepburn, Spencer Tracy, Sidney Poitier, and Katherine Houghton. The daughter of a white liberal family brings home her fiancé, a talented black doctor, throwing her family into turmoil.

In the Heat of the Night, 1967, directed by Norman Jewison and starring Sidney Poitier, Rod Steiger, Warren Oates, and Lee Grant. A black Philadelphia detective passing through is detained by a reluctant police chief and is asked to help solve the crime of a rich man killed in a small Mississippi town.

Ragtime, 1981, directed by Milos Forman and starring Howard E. Rollins, Jr., Mary Steenburgen, James Cagney, and Donald O'Connor. The story of a middle-class American family in 1906 swept into scandal is placed side by side with the tragedy of a proud young black man.

Zoot Suit, 1981, directed by Luis Valdez and starring Edward James Olmos, Daniel Valdez, and Tyne Daly. The true story of a Mexican-American in the 1940s wrongfully accused of murder.

Mississippi Burning, 1988, directed by Alan Parker and starring Gene Hackman, Willem Dafoe, Francis McDormand, and Stephen Tobolowsky. Three activists disappear in 1964

Mississippi, and the FBI is called in to investigate, only to find the local authorities stonewalling.

MEMORABLE WAR FILMS

The consistent theme in these stories is that no one ever really wins, especially not the little guy who holds the rifle.

All Quiet on the Western Front, 1930, directed by Lewis Milestone and starring Lew Ayers, John Wray, and Beryl Mercer. Several German youths are convinced to join the effort in World War I, only to encounter horrors that will change them forever.

For Whom the Bell Tolls, 1943, directed by Sam Wood and starring Gary Cooper, Ingrid Bergman, and Arturo de Cordova. An American schoolteacher goes to Spain to fight against the Fascists in this great adaptation of the Hemingway novel.

The Best Years of Our Lives, 1946, directed by William Wyler and starring Fredric March, Myrna Loy, Dana Andrews,

Soldiers who find home a difficult place are the subjects of William Wyler's moving *The Best Years of Our Lives* (1946).

Teresa Wright, and Harold Russell. Three World War II veterans return home and face the difficulty of readjusting to the civilian world.

The Deer Hunter, 1978, directed by Michael Cimino and starring Robert DeNiro, Christopher Walken, and Meryl Streep. Three midwestern steel workers go to Vietnam, and their war experiences alter not only their lives, but those left behind.

Apocalypse Now, 1979, directed by Francis Ford Coppola and starring Marlon Brando, Martin Sheen, Robert Duvall, Lawrence Fishburne, and Harrison Ford. An army captain is sent upriver into Cambodia to kill a renegade colonel, but things get darker as he travels.

Gallipoli, 1981, directed by Peter Weir and starring Mel Gibson, Mark Lee, and Bill Kerr. Two friends join Australian light horse cavalry and stumble into one of the most tragic debacles of military history.

The Killing Fields, 1984, directed by Roland Joffe and starring Sam Waterston, Haing S. Ngor, and John Malkovich. After the fall of Saigon, western journalists escaped but left Cambodian interpreters behind to be imprisoned, tortured, and killed by the Khmer Rouge.

Platoon, 1986, directed by Oliver Stone and starring Charlie Sheen, Willem Dafoe, and Tom Berenger. One of the most graphic looks at what many Vietnam soldiers went through during the war.

Richard III, 1995, directed by Richard Loncraine and starring Ian McKellen, Annette Bening, and Maggie Smith. This updated version of the William Shakespeare play about the deformed usurper Richard of Gloucester is set in Nazi-esque London. Provocative on a variety of levels, unlike most attempts of this kind.

Saving Private Ryan, 1998, directed by Steven Spielberg and starring Tom Hanks, Matt Damon, Edward Burns, and Tom Sizemore. Just after D-Day in World War II, an army captain and his squad are given a special assignment—to find and bring back safely a private whose three brothers have already died in battle.

FILMS ABOUT LIFE BEHIND BARS

These next films look at how both innocent people and criminals are treated once they are behind bars.

I Am a Fugitive from a Chain Gang, 1932, directed by Mervyn LeRoy and starring Paul Muni, Allen Jenkins, and

Clint Eastwood suffers the humiliations of confinement in Don Siegel's *Escape from Alcatraz* (1979).

Helen Vinson. A World War I veteran is falsely convicted of a crime and sentenced to a brutal Georgia chain gang.

Birdman of Alcatraz, 1962, directed by John Frankenheimer and starring Burt Lancaster, Karl Malden, and Telly Savalas. Two-time killer Robert Stroud is in Alcatraz for life and while there becomes one of the world's foremost authorities on birds.

Cool Hand Luke, 1967, directed by Stuart Rosenberg and starring Paul Newman, George Kennedy, and Strother Martin. A new prisoner sweating out his sentence in a prison farm refuses to let authorities break his spirit.

Escape from Alcatraz, 1979, directed by Don Siegel and starring Clint Eastwood, Danny Glover, and Fred Ward. Only one man made a successful escape from "The Rock," and this is his story.

The Jericho Mile, 1979, directed by Michael Mann and starring Peter Strauss, Roger E. Mosley, and Brian Dennehy. A prisoner who loves running gets a chance at the Olympics.

Breaker Morant, 1980, directed by Bruce Beresford and starring Edward Woodward, Jack Thompson, and Bryan Brown. Based on a true story, three Australian soldiers stationed in South Africa in 1901 during the Boer War are falsely accused of murdering several prisoners in their care.

Brubaker, 1980, directed by Stuart Rosenberg and starring Robert Redford, Jane Alexander, and Yaphet Kotto. A warden takes over a state prison and against overwhelming odds tries to reform the dehumanizing situation.

In the Name of the Father, 1993, directed by Jim Sheridan and starring Daniel Day-Lewis, Pete Postlethwaite, and Emma Thompson. Based on a true story, Gerry Conlon and the Guildford Four are falsely imprisoned in 1974 by the British for an IRA bombing, but a woman lawyer believes Conlon is innocent and fights for his release.

Andersonville, 1995, directed by John Frankenheimer and starring Frederic Forrest, Cliff DeYoung, and William H. Macy. The notorious Andersonville facility was built for 8,000 Union prisoners, but more than 32,000 were sent there.

Paradise Road, 1997, directed by Bruce Beresford and starring Glenn Close, Francis McDormand, and Pauline Collins. During World War II, a group of American, British, and Australian women leave Singapore. When their ship is bombed, they end up in Sumatra as prisoners of the Japanese.

FILMS ABOUT THE CORRUPTION OF POWER

These films show what happens when people who are voted to hold office or fill other trusted positions misuse that trust.

Mutiny on the Bounty, 1935, directed by Frank Lloyd and starring Clark Gable, Franchot Tone, and Charles Laughton. This is the first retelling of the story of the famous mutiny on

Clark Gable as Fletcher Christian protects the overthrown Captain Bligh played by Charles Laughton in Frank Lloyd's *Mutiny on the Bounty* (1935).

the *HMS Bounty*, with memorable performances by Gable as Fletcher Christian and Laughton as the stiff Captain Bligh.

Mr. Smith Goes to Washington, 1939, directed by Frank Capra and starring Jimmy Stewart, Jean Arthur, Claude Rains, and Thomas Mitchell. A truly great film about an idealistic small-town man appointed to replace a Senator, who finds himself the pawn of a political machine once he's in Washington.

The Last Hurrah, 1958, directed by John Ford and starring Spencer Tracy, Basil Rathbone, and Jeffrey Hunter. An aging Irish-American mayor goes for one last election but has some heavy corrupt dealings to overcome.

Advise and Consent, 1962, directed by Otto Preminger and starring Don Murray, Charles Laughton, Henry Fonda, and Betty White. The President makes a choice for Secretary of State that creates a political dogfight in the Senate.

Seven Days in May, 1964, directed by John Frankenheimer and starring Burt Lancaster, Kirk Douglas, Edmond O'Brien, Fredric March, and Ava Gardner. An American general feels his commander-in-chief is too weak; so he plots a military takeover of the government.

All the President's Men, 1976, directed by Alan J. Pakula and starring Robert Redford, Dustin Hoffman, and Jason Robards, Jr. The portrayal of the scandal of the Watergate break-in and how two *Washington Post* reporters broke the story against overwhelming odds.

Above the Law, 1988, directed by Andrew Davis and starring Steven Segal, Pam Grier, Henry Silva, and Sharon Stone. An ultra-secret government agency is doing illegal operations worldwide and uses greed, cover-ups, torture, and murder to make sure no one stops them.

City Hall, 1995, directed by Harold Becker and starring Al Pacino, John Cusack, and Bridget Fonda. New York City's deputy mayor, investigating three different murders, uncovers corruption that will embarrass many city officials.

My Fellow Americans, 1996, directed by Peter Segal and starring James Garner, Jack Lemmon, Dan Aykroyd, Lauren Bacall, and Sela Ward. Two former Presidents who are as different as day and night are compelled to join forces to clear their names when the present President frames them in a scandal.

L.A. Confidential, 1997, directed by Curtis Hanson and starring Kevin Spacey, Kim Basinger, Russell Crowe, and Danny DeVito. In 1950s Los Angeles several police officers uncover corruption, prostitution, graft, and other vices that will put their lives in danger.

VISIONS OF THE FUTURE

These films are Hollywood's look at what the future may or may not hold for mankind.

Metropolis, 1926, directed by Fritz Lang and starring Brigitte Helm, Alfred Able, and Fritz Rasp. A great German expressionist looks at how future technology will affect the earth. See it in a restored print.

Things to Come, 1936, directed by William Cameron Menzies and starring Raymond Massey, Margaretta Scott, Ralph Richardson, and Cedric Hardwicke. Scientists try to rebuild the world after wars and other calamities have affected the planet.

Fahrenheit 451, 1966, directed by Francois Truffaut and starring Oskar Werner, Julie Christie, and Anton Diffring. Firemen burn books in this futuristic nightmare. Based on the Ray Bradbury novel.

2001: A Space Odyssey, 1968, directed by Stanley Kubrick and starring Keir Dullea, Gary Lockwood, and William Sylvester. Man is on his way to Jupiter, but there is a malfunction on the Hal 9000 computer, and the crew is in deadly peril.

Soylent Green, 1973, directed by Richard Fleischer and starring Charlton Heston, Leigh Taylor-Young, and Edward G. Robinson. A twenty-first-century police detective investigates a murder and discovers corporate corruption of the most horrible kind.

A Boy and His Dog, 1975, directed by L. Q. Jones and starring Don Johnson, Susanne Benton, and Jason Robards, Jr. Quirky yet fine film set in 2024 and involving a young man and his telepathic dog who roam a wasted earth to find shelter and food.

Blade Runner, 1982, directed by Ridley Scott and starring Harrison Ford, Rutger Hauser, and Sean Young. It's Los Angeles in the twenty-first century, and a cop is out after destructive androids. A modern classic with stunning, if at times upsetting, visuals.

The Road Warrior, 1981, directed by George Miller and starring Mel Gibson, Bruce Spence, and Vernon Wells. This is the second of the three "Mad Max" films, set after nuclear war has left Australia a wasteland ruled by killer gangs. Gibson created a genre with his role.

1984, 1984, directed by Michael Radford and starring John Hurt, Richard Burton, and Suzanna Hamilton. An illegal love affair brings on the wrath of Big Brother in this still terrifying George Orwell nightmare.

12 Monkeys, 1995, directed by Terry Gilliam and starring Bruce Willis, Madeline Stowe, and Brad Pitt. Forty years after a plague wiped out 99 percent of mankind, a criminal is sent back in time to find how the plague started.

SILENT FILMS

Film reached remarkable maturity very quickly, and in the 1920s films of enduring power and beauty were already being made. These are among the best.

Broken Blossoms, 1919, directed by D. W. Griffith and starring Lillian Gish, Donald Barthelmess, and Donald Crisp. This may not be pioneer Griffith's best, but it is arguably his most lyrical and memorable film, a story of an abused child who bonds with a lonely Chinese man.

Nanook of the North, 1922, directed by Robert Flaherty. This documentary of Eskimos fighting for survival in the far north set the standard for all documentaries to follow and continues to appeal.

He Who Gets Slapped, 1924, directed by Victor Seastrom and starring Lon Chaney, Norma Shearer, John Gilbert, and Tully Marshall. A scientist becomes a clown in order to hide from his past, only to fall in love with a beautiful young performer in the circus.

Sunrise, 1927, directed by F. W. Murnau and starring George O'Brien, Janet Gaynor, Bodil Rosing, and Margaret Livingston. Beautiful to behold; a moving story of a country man led by a vixen to attempt to murder his wife.

The General, 1927, directed by Buster Keaton and starring Buster Keaton, Marion Mack, Glen Cavender, Jim Farley, and Joseph Keaton. Remarkably authentic backgrounds for this classic Keaton comedy about a stolen train in the Civil War make this more than simply funny.

The Crowd, 1928, directed by King Vidor and starring Eleanor Boardman, James Murray, Bert Roach, and Lucy Beaumont. A beautiful drama about the progress of an ill-fated yet ordinary married couple.

The Docks of New York, 1928, directed by Josef Von Sternberg and starring George Bancroft, Betty Compson, Olga Baclanova, and Mitchell Lewis. A gorgeously photographed story of a rough ship stoker who marries a poor woman only to find himself falling in love with her.

Street Angel, 1928, directed by Frank Borzage and starring

Charlie Chaplin's tramp falls in love with a beautiful blind
woman played by Virginia Cherrill in Chaplin's poignant
masterpiece *City Lights* (1931).

Janet Gaynor, Charles Farrell, Guido Trento, and Natalie
Kingston. A poor girl on the run from the police joins the circus
and becomes the inspiration for a young painter—romanticism
at its very best.

City Lights, 1931, directed by Charlie Chaplin and starring
Charlie Chaplin, Virginia Cherrill, Harry Myers, and Hank
Mann. This eloquent and masterful Chaplin comedy about a little tramp trying to court a blind girl who thinks he is a million-
aire ends unforgettably.

Tabu, 1931, directed by F. W. Murnau and starring Anna
Chevalier, Matahi, Hitu, Jules, and Jean. Shot in Tahiti by the
great Robert Flaherty, this is the romantic tale of a pearl fisher-
man who falls in love with a cursed native girl.

Some Recommended Reading

The Film Encyclopedia, Ephraim Katz, 1998, HarperCollins. This invaluable resource contains informational articles on a broad range of subjects related to film and filmmaking. Carefully researched, insightful, and well-written.

Halliwell's Filmgoer's Companion, edited by John Walker, 2000, HarperCollins. This book is the academics' choice for an alphabetical source listing of movie titles, actors, and categories. A separate section lists Academy Award winners, winners of British Academy of Films and Television Arts (BAFTA), winners of the Golden Bear Award from the Berlin Film Festival, winners of the Palme d'Or from the Cannes Film Festival, and winners of the Golden Lion of St. Mark Award from the Venice Film Festival. A separate section lists film books and periodicals, film guides on CD-ROM, and a brief history of the cinema and contributions made by various countries to the art form of films.

A History of Narrative Film, David A. Cook, 1996, Norton. A jawbreaker of a history of film from the beginnings in the late nineteenth-century. For the detail-minded and serious student only.

Hollywood Film Genres, Thomas Schatz, 1981, McGraw-Hill. The best discussion available of why certain American film genres have become popular from one of the most articulate scholars in the business. The book's only flaw is that it is twenty years old and therefore does not address recent trends.

How to Read a Film, James Monaco, 1999, Oxford. Another academic jawbreaker, but a great resource if you want to study further the science of film interpretation.

Disney A to Z, Dave Smith, 1998, Hyperion. An alphabetical sourcebook on the various films, theme parks, and commodities that are part of the Walt Disney organization. Easy to read, with a lot of photos and trivia that make for interesting reading, especially if you have kids addicted to the films.

Videohound's Golden Movie Retriever, 2000, Visible Ink. This book, updated yearly, lists 23,000 films alphabetically. Included are ratings, release dates, running times, cast members, directors, award nominations, and awards won. It also contains an alphabetical listing of over 40,000 actors, directors, screenwriters, and composers.

100 Best Movies for Kids, Jeffrey Lyons, 1996, Simon & Schuster. This book lists worthy titles picked out by PBS *Sneak Preview* host and film reviewer for ABC's *World News Now*, Jeffrey Lyons. The titles are in alphabetical order with category, cast, director, running time, release date, rating, production company, suggested age group, plot synopsis, and background. This book may offer parents needed help in finding quality films.

Conclusion

In a recent review of the Ridley Scott film *Gladiator*, a local writer suggested that twenty-first century Americans might find strong similarities between the hunger for spectacle in ancient Roman culture and that of our own. At first I brushed off that comment, but then I happened to see the Mel Gibson vehicle *Patriot* with my wife, during which we were treated to the experience of a cannonball aimed straight at the camera, which then took off the head of a Revolutionary soldier. Just the kind of entertainment a Christian man and his wife should enjoy.

We have become in large measure a culture addicted to spectacle, unable to discern any longer what is worthwhile and what is debasing. As such, we should be haunted by the implicit warnings of Paul's description of human culture in decline in Romans 1: "Therefore, God gave them over in the sinful desires of their hearts to . . . Because of this, God gave them over to . . ." (vv. 24, 26).

It is imperative that the Church read correctly the signs of the times and respond wisely, particularly to those aspects of culture most central to the hearts and minds of ordinary people. The Church needs to examine contemporary film carefully and to speak with authority.

This little book is an attempt to encourage such a response. We have not addressed all questions related to contemporary film in these pages. What we have offered are some basic principles and personal observations drawn from years of our own experiences wrestling with the medium of film. If our points are invalid or our observations inaccurate, we hope that those who follow may better express the truth. In fact, it will be a measure of our success to discover in years to come that our book has lost relevance due to a wave of great Christian thought and writing on the subject of film. Of the points we have made along the way, the following are the most significant.

First, *Christians must get involved in all aspects of the film industry and find ways to use that medium to honor God and advance the Gospel.* There are certainly times to avoid film altogether, as one would flee idolatry; but while there is opportunity to use the medium through wise criticism, production, and distribution, that opportunity should be embraced. Perhaps the most effective way to do this is to encourage young men and women of faith to study film and enter the industry. Christian colleges and universities should lead the way in this endeavor by offering top-notch programs in film production and film studies.

Second, *individual Christians who watch film should find the means to educate themselves and their children about film.* This point is predicated upon the understanding that film is a complex medium that requires some training to unwrap. One of the great scandals of modern Christianity is that believers have allowed themselves to be subjected to hours upon hours of popular media—film, TV, music, etc.—with very little instruction regarding how to respond. We have assimilated the cultural notion that entertainment is spiritually and morally innocent. It is not.

Third, *films need to be evaluated according to the twin standards of artistic excellence and truthfulness.* We must learn to discern between the excellent and the wretched when it comes to art, and Scripture exhorts us to embrace the excellent and the beautiful. Likewise, we should measure all statements and representations against the truth of Scripture—particularly regarding the nature of humanity and human redemption through Christ. Satan is the father of all lies. Jesus is the Way and the Truth.

Fourth, *the popularity of certain kinds of film reveals much about the longings of the human heart in general, as well as particular cultural and historical moments.* Film genres may be predictable and intellectually unchallenging; yet, their continuing popularity provides us a way to understand the people around us, and ourselves as well. The popularity of the western and then its demise, the rise of the action thriller, the persistence of sentimental romance—all of these tendencies give us opportunity as Christians to establish points of contact between the culture in which we move and the Gospel that we carry.

Fifth, *the influence of Christianity upon film has already been profound.* The tendency of films with spiritual import to draw upon the Christian tradition, particularly Christian liturgics, and the ongoing saga of the biblical film suggests that the way has already been paved for a new Christian cinema. Those who want to use existing films for the purpose of teaching or encouragement will with some guidance find a large number of possible titles. Despite recent discouraging tendencies in Hollywood film, Christians can take heart at the tremendous influence that believers have been able to have in the industry in the past. Some of the greatest works of Christian art in the twentieth century are films like *Diary of a Country Priest, Open City, On the Waterfront, Black Robe, Andrei Rublev,* and *A Farewell to Arms.* As the larger Body of Christ, we should make a greater effort to recognize and celebrate such works.

Sixth, *the wide range of films produced in the past hundred years offers manifold opportunity for Christians to enter into dialogue with the larger culture.* Be it through discussions of the evolving family in America, the nature of the Holocaust, race relations, or war, film offers concrete illustrations of contemporary ideas that linger in the mind and can be addressed critically. There is little question that most Americans, for example, would have lost sight of the importance of D-Day if not for the film

Saving Private Ryan. Even films that challenge the teachings of the Church on one issue or another, like *Thelma and Louise* or *The Piano* on gender roles, offer opportunities for Christians to speak that might not otherwise have been offered. God at times strikes a straight blow with a crooked stick.

If there is more to say on these preliminary matters regarding Christianity and film, we trust it will come from those who review and respond to this book. All dialogue that leads us toward a greater understanding is welcome.

Peter Fraser

Index

Note: This index includes movie titles from Chapter 8 ("A Reviewer's Guide by Vernon Edwin Neal"), but not the names of actors and actresses, directors, etc.